Mexico's Copper Canyon Country

P9-DER-996

Mexico's Copper Canyon Country

A Hiking and
Backpacking Guide to
Tarahumara-land

M. John Fayhee

CORDILLERA PRESS, INC.
Publishers in the Rockies

Library of Congress Cataloging-in-Publication Data
Fayhee, M. John.
   Mexico's Copper Canyon country : a hiking and backpacking guide to Tarahumara-land / M. John Fayhee.
      p.   cm.
   Includes bibliographical references.
   ISBN 0-917895-28-2
   1. Hiking — Mexico — Sierra Madre — Guide-books.
   2. Backpacking — Mexico — Sierra Madre — Guide-books.
   3. Sierra Madre Range (Mexico) — Description and travel — Guide-books.
   I. Title.
   GV199.44.M62S544   1989
   917.2'75 — dc20   89-22238
                                                                                      CIP

First Printing
   1   2   3   4   5   6   7   8   9

Printed in the United States of America.

WARNING: Backcountry travel is a dangerous activity. Users of this guide participate in backpacking and hiking activities solely at their own risk.

NOTE: Parts of Chapters 5 and 6 first appeared in the November 1987 issue of *Backpacker* magazine in an article titled, "Bottoming Out in Mexico." Other parts of Chapter 6 first appeared in the September 1987 issue of *Rocky Mountain Sports and Fitness* in an article titled, "Beating Feet and Pounding Brews with the Tarahumaras." Parts of several chapters appeared in the May-June 1989 issue of *Summit*.

Front Cover Photograph   *All cover photographs by Gay Gangel-Fayhee.*
   On the trail to Pamachi.   *Interior photographs not otherwise credited,*
Back Cover Photographs   *by M. John Fayhee.*
   Top: *Hiking down from Divisadero.*
   Middle: *Tarahumara girl near Cusarare Falls.*
   Below, Left: *Copper Canyon Lodge.*
   Below, Right: *Cusarare Falls.*

Design & Typography (Cover & Interior)
   Richard M. Kohen · Shadow Canyon Graphics - Evergreen, Colorado

Cordillera Press, Inc.
Post Office Box 3699
Evergreen, Colorado 80439
(303) 670-3010

Contents

Gay Gangel-Fayhee on trail to Pamachi above Urique River.

To
Chuck and Marian Gangel,
of Cañon City, Colorado
— parents-in-law extraordinaire —
for their support,
their interest and,
most of all,
their eldest daughter.

And to Jay Scott,
of Silver City, New Mexico,
who kept me focused,
and thus alive,
during those six crazy days
in Tararecua Canyon.

*Here nature
chose to think
like a man.*

Antonin Artaud
The Peyote Dance

Tarahumaras on rock outcrop above Urique Canyon
near the great bend of the Urique River.
Note traditional dress of Tara on left.

What This Book Is, And What It Is Not

I'm sitting here in this little drinking establishment in the town where I live — a place with an antique Harley-Davidson hanging on the wall above my shoulder. Maps of the Copper Canyon region — Tarahumara-land I call it because of the Tarahumara Indians there — are spread from one end of this beer-stained table to the other and I'm staring down at them, feeling a little stunned.

As far as I can tell from the maps at hand, there are *at least* 75 potential multi-day backpacking trips to be had thereabouts — to say nothing of the potential for one-nighters and day-hikes. In this guide, I describe a mere dozen or so routes I have personally hiked, as well as several more that I have reliable information about. All told, less than 20 trips out of those 75-plus.

In my own defense, I have put in a *lot* of backpacking and done a *lot* of hiking in Copper Canyon Country. But, the place is so immense that, after four separate trips covering many months, I realize that I have only scratched the surface. Which isn't necessarily bad.

Most of us are familiar with areas that have been guide-booked to death. The Appalachian Trail corridor comes to mind. There exists a series of A.T. guidebooks that are so detailed you literally know your route in tenth-of-a-mile increments before you even hoist your pack.

In my forays into Copper Canyon Country, I have found that

one of the things that attracts people most about this place is the fact that it has not been guide-booked into a catatonic stupor. At the same time, just about every person armed with backpacks and boots I have met in Tarahumara-land has lamented the fact that — until now — there has been zilch in the way of informational resources targeted towards backpackers and day-hikers. These people were simply looking for a place to start — a couple of generalized recommendations, a few bewares and a little insight into the culture of their Tarahumara hosts — written by and for backcountry users.

I've tried to meet that need without destroying the ambience of the unknown that is one of Copper Canyon Country's most tantalizing attributes. So, that's what this book is — something in between an agonizingly detailed guidebook and nothing. An introduction to hiking in Copper Canyon Country. A primer, as it were, to a special land and its special people.

I try to point you in the right direction with the kinds of hints — regarding gear, weather, trail conditions, local culture, particularly nice or not-so-nice areas — that you would lay on a fellow adventurer if you commenced to swapping backpacking tales over a cold beer. And, while I'm at it, I'll toss in a few of the yarns I've been known to spin.

But, understand this. Most of the Copper Canyon region is very rough territory. It is generally well-mapped, but not perfectly. It is very isolated. There are no search and rescue teams. Medical facilities are few, far between and primitive.

This is an area where you must have a firm understanding of your personal limitations as a backcountry user, both physically and mentally. If you know what you can and cannot handle — whether you are a world-class wilderness jock with the dust of Patagonia and Borneo on your boots or a relative neophyte whose big trip was a weekend in the Catskills — then this book will hook you up with the type of hike you will enjoy, whether you are looking to stretch your limits or not.

What I will not do, is lead you by the hand and tell you to take a left at the big tree with the knot in it, walk 17.23 feet and there, under the third-shortest bush, is a seep spring. If you *need* this kind of information, perhaps it would be better to chalk up a little more backcountry experience before you cruise down to

Tarahumara-land.

And, if you just *want* that kind of information, know up front that the very nature of Copper Canyon Country makes giving specific trail and distance statistics tough. I talk about average hours required to knock off a given stretch of trail. Most of these times are based on the time it took my wife and I to hike that particular stretch. (We are not particularly fast walkers, we are not in particularly great shape, and we usually carry too much weight.) I have no choice about this. The trails in Tarahumara-land are not marked, let alone measured, and topographical variations and switchbacks make it frequently difficult to even guesstimate distances.

If you feel more comfortable with detailed, comprehensive information and you still want to visit the area, just hire a guide. I list several in the next chapter and note those instances where they might be helpful. For those of you who feel you can handle Copper Canyon Country without a guide, I make a number of assumptions — and they are a good way to gauge whether or not you have enough experience to be trekking around these parts in the first place. I assume you will:

- purchase maps of the area you intend to traverse — listed at the end of each chapter — and become as familiar as possible with the local topography;
- know how to use both the compass you will bring and those maps;
- arrive in fairly good shape with fairly reliable gear;
- inform a responsible party of your itinerary;
- have a good understanding of first aid;
- respect and prepare for the potential harshness of the climate — both hot and cold;
- learn as much Spanish as possible before arriving in Mexico;
- be willing to share your cigars if you meet me on the trail; and
- respect the Tarahumara and Mexican cultures at least as much as you pretend to respect you own.

I will give you enough information to get you started on *your* trip into Tarahumara-land — *your* personal exploration of one of the most beautiful and least-explored areas in North America. Remember though, in order for your trip to be successful —

however *you* define that — you need to rely not on me, but on you. I will feel much better about my efforts if I know that you've spent less time with your eyes focused on these pages and more time with them focused on the trail.

In these pages, I will introduce you to my attractive and provocative friend. If you want to get to know my friend better, you will need to come up with your own seduction lines.

It's better that way.

◄►

Hikers near Tararecua Canyon.

Nuts & Bolts

I read one time that Copper Canyon Country was not such a hot place for backpacking due to a lack of clearly marked and defined trails. Seriously, I laughed so hard I spilled a Carta Blanca all over my lap. The statement proves that you should always be somewhat skeptical of subjective viewpoints, mine included.

First of all, lots of folks I know prefer to hike in places with a *conspicuous* lack of clearly marked trails. But, more importantly, the statement is patently false. Copper Canyon Country is criss-crossed by a network of paths that, while not marked in the sense that we consider paths "marked" in Yosemite, are as obvious as stink in a small tent. I mean, this place is populated by 50,000 Tarahumara Indians who, with very limited exceptions, walk or run everywhere they go. And they have been doing so for centuries. Taras follow the same routes from one *ranchito* to the next and back again and again. These footpaths serve as the Tarahumara interstate highway system, and, consequently, in many areas they are worn down several feet.

As well, they often connect places a backpacker would want to visit, like between Panalachi and Tehuirichi (Chapter 15) or between Batopilas and Munérachi (Chapter 14). This is not to say that there aren't plenty of areas in Tarahumara-land void of trails. The lower reaches of Tararecua Canyon, for instance. (Chapter 5).

Tara trails connect villages and *ranchitos*. Though it is my observation that Taras generally enjoy walking through the beauteous region they inhabit, they don't often take strolls solely for the sake of sight-seeing. If you find yourself in an area that is not between two points that the Taras have reason to walk back and forth between, then the best you can hope for are meandering goat paths, which are a serious drag to walk on — unless you are a goat.

This is not to say, as well, that many of the more frequently used Tara footpaths don't have their "captivating" sections. I have followed trails for hours that would do the Great Smokies proud, only to find myself suddenly facing an advanced rock-climbing move, 300 feet up on some crumbly cliff in order to proceed one millimeter further.

But, by and large, if it begins as a major trail, it will likely stay a major trail — at least until it terminates at the place all of these Taras have been cruising to for hundreds of years. Which may or may not be the same place you want to go. But this has to do with the more-rugged parts of Copper Canyon Country. Much of the area we'll be dealing with in this book is rolling, high-valley terrain around the deepest canyons — territory no more fearsome than the Berkshires, and twice, maybe three times, as beautiful.

Which gets us to nomenclature. When we talk about "Copper Canyon Country" — *Las Barrancas del Cobre* in local parlance — we are not being very specific. There are no signs welcoming you and, if there were, the argument would rage for decades as to where they should be erected. You may see some references to "Copper Canyon National Park." This is a myth. There is simply no such thing.

While there is such a specific beast as "Copper Canyon," cartographers and others who spend time pondering this sort of thing are not totally in agreement as to what it is, or where it begins and ends. There is a certain amount of confusion because of the pluralization of the Spanish name one frequently hears for the area: *Las Barrancas del Cobre*, giving the impression, at least in translation, that there are several canyons in the vicinity sharing a common appellation, along with common degrees of renown and grandeur. *Barranca* is Spanish for "canyon," though geologists generally consider it a specific type of canyon — one in which the walls descend in a series of benches rather than in one gigantic vertical plunge. *Cobre* is Spanish for copper.

The English translation is almost always, simply, the singular, "Copper Canyon," giving the impression that there is one canyon that surpasses all others nearby in splendor, depth and impor-

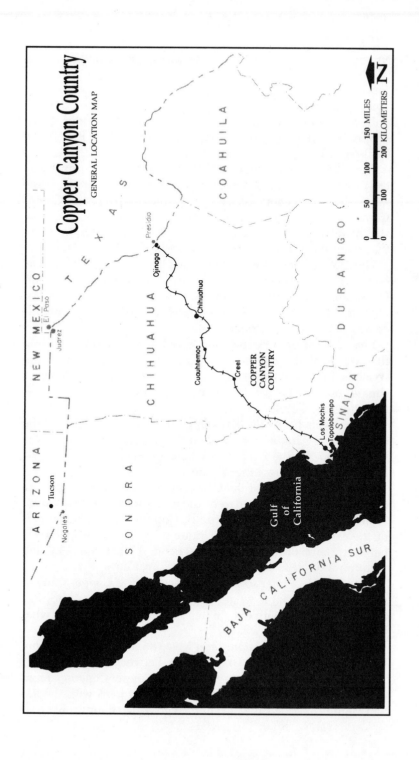

Copper Canyon Country

GENERAL LOCATION MAP

tance. This perspective is further reinforced by the fact that the only canyon most visitors see is that which is most often called simply "Copper Canyon" — the huge canyon of the Rio Urique (OO-ree-kay).

The 1:250,000-scale topographic map of the area, printed by the Direccion General de Geografia del Territorio Nacional, designates the canyon formed by the Urique, "Barranca *el* Cobre" from the Umira (sometimes spelled "Humira") Bridge downstream to where the Urique is joined by Arroyo Hondo. From that point on, it is called Barranca Urique.

The 1:50,000-scale topos, which are part of the Mexican Defense Department series, call the canyon "Barranca *del* Cobre" from Umira Bridge to the junction of the Urique and Arroyo Hondo, where this essentially continuous canyon suddenly becomes "Barranca del Urique."

I have heard from people who have lived their whole lives in this area that there is no one "Copper Canyon," that all the canyons in Tarahumara-land, a canyon area of about 10,000 square miles — are part of a system of canyons known as "Las Barrancas del Cobre."

Other locals have said that Copper Canyon is that part of the canyon of the Urique from the Umira Bridge downstream to the "great bend" of the Urique — where Tararecua Canyon of the Rio San Ignacio enters the Urique.

Dr. Robert Schmidt of the University of Texas at El Paso, who has prepared a popular map of the area for sale at the Mission Store in Creel, says that historically, Copper Canyon is that part of the canyon formed by the Urique near El Tejabán, which is between Umira Bridge and the great bend. A lot of copper mining went on around El Tejabán back in colonial days.

In this book, I refer to the entire area as the Copper Canyon *system*, because that is what people know this area as and, like they say in eastern Virginia, "if that's what you call it, that's what its name is."

Then, to avoid confusion, or at least to ignore any confusion, I call the canyon of the Urique River between its source near Norogachi downriver to the great bend, "Copper Canyon." From that point downriver all the way to where it joins with the Rio San Miguel to become the Rio Fuerte, I go with Urique Canyon.

Anyway, we're talking about a system of canyons that rivals any in the world in total square mileage, overall depth of individual canyons, displacement, beauty, ruggedness, the whole nine yards. The system, depending on where you want to draw the line, consists of at least seven significant canyons: Urique, Copper, Batopilas, Sinforosa Canyon of the Rio Verde, Tararecua Canyon of the Rio San Ignacio, Cusarare and the Conchos. All of these are deep, with the exception of the Conchos, which is the only major river in Tarahumara-land on the eastern side of the Continental Divide. Urique Canyon at the village of Urique is about 1,800 meters (5,900 feet) deep, as is Sinforosa Canyon near Guachochi. Batopilas Canyon at the town of Batopilas is about 2,100 meters (6,900 feet) deep, depending on where you measure it from.

I should point out here that there is no set system for measuring the depth of canyons or gorges. Do you measure them from the closest mountaintop to river level? From the highest rim to river level? From the lowest rim? How about averaging the distance from each rim to the river? I have researched this in some depth and, according to everyone I have talked with, including employees of the United States Geological Survey, the Guinness Book of World Records and the National Geographic Society, no one, or no entity, has ever settled this question one way or the other.

The most persuasive arguments I have heard on this came from a couple of "uncredentialed" folks, who just happen to be the foremost canyoneers in the world. They argue that we should use the rim-averaging method. I think, when attempting to compare canyons, we should measure their displacement — that is, how much dirt would it take to fill it back up? This takes care of comparison of width, depth and length in one fell swoop.

The canyons of the Urique and the Rio Verde are, as far as I can tell, the second-and third-deepest in North America — the deepest being Hell's Canyon on the border of Idaho and Oregon with a depth of about 7,900 feet.

Copper Canyon Country is located roughly halfway between Chihuahua City, Chihuahua, which is about 200 miles south of El Paso, Texas, and Los Mochis, Sinaloa, which is about 300 miles south of Nogales, Arizona. Almost all of Copper Canyon Country is located in the Mexican state of Chihuahua.

Traveling In Mexico

It amazes me that there are still people who are scared to travel south of the border. Visions of the "we don't need no stinking badges" scene in "Treasure of the Sierra Madre" still affect many otherwise intelligent gringos — the universal and by no means derogatory term by which all Anglos are known.

Mexico, my friends, is a very easy place to be. Gone are the days of freaks in VW vans getting stomped by the *federales*. At least for the most part. I have never had anything even approaching a bad experience in Mexico, except maybe that one time I had an M-16 stuck up my right nostril. But that was just a small misunderstanding, easily rectified. And I have never even heard a first-hand story any more intense than someone having to pay a few bucks to a corrupt cop.

This is not to say that there aren't dangers in our sister country, especially in the drug cultivation regions of Culiacan, Guerrero, Colima, Michoacan, Jalisco and Sinaloa. Nightmares to be had in Mexico include various types of assault by private citizens and various degrees of hassles by gendarmes of whatever species. I don't know that there's much more to say than, "Be careful and keep your eyes peeled." The same advice I would give a Mexican planning to visit New York City.

Just remember, keep your cool if the scene gets tense. If you have a problem with the police, keep a smile on your face. Be verbally deferential. It will not help matters if you lose your temper and get threatening. And of course, the more Spanish you know, the better.

Mexicans are wonderful people. They love their country and are usually flattered that you have decided to pay them a visit. Most will go out of their way to help you at the drop of a hat.

Okay, technicalities.

At the border, you will need to get a tourist card, which is free and usually good for however long you ask for, up to six months. You will need to show proof of national origin. While in theory, you can use a birth certificate or voter registration card, you are well advised to get a passport and bring it with you. I have heard that border officials are beginning to lose patience with voter registration cards because they have no photograph. If you don't have a passport, your local post office can start you in the right direction. Allow six weeks for the paperwork to be processed — a cost of $42 in 1989.

If you are just visiting a border town, you won't need a tourist card. If you are going into the interior, you must pick one up at the border. Unlike the U.S., you cross into Mexican border towns — on foot — without being stopped. You have to go out of your way to get officially processed into the country. Immigration offices are located at all border crossings and processing usually takes only a few minutes. If you are traveling through Mexico to another country, you will need to buy a trans-migration visa as well.

About thirty miles south of every border town, there are customs and immigration stops. If you lack a tourist card, you will be sent back to the border to rectify the situation.

It is important that you don't lose your tourist card because, on your way back into the States, you may be asked to surrender it. Also, if you get into any sort of legal flap while in Mexico, you will have to produce your card.

In all likelihood, your gear won't be checked at the border unless you drive into the country. When you check your gear at the bus or train station, the local customs agent (*aduana*) may ask you to open your pack. You are not being hassled here. This is normal procedure. Generally speaking, Mexican customs and immigration employees are very pleasant and efficient.

If you drive into Mexico, things are slightly more complicated. You must have Mexican insurance, which you can buy at most American border towns. Sanborn's is the big company. This is important. Your U.S. coverage is not valid in Mexico. For full coverage, expect to pay about $4 a day. The Mexican government strictly controls insurance rates, so you don't have to worry about getting ripped off by the carrier.

Also, expect to get searched a little more thoroughly if you drive into the country. Mexican customs officials are generally looking for consumer goods that, they fear, you may be looking to peddle. So expect scrutiny if you try to bring 30 VCRs in. They are also serious business about guns.

Road quality varies from excellent to stuff that looks like the surface of Mars. The main highways are all good.

The main problem with driving in Mexico is gas. You can purchase only terrible-quality, very low-octane gas only from nationally owned Pemex stations. Once you get off the main highways, you will be unable to buy unleaded (*sinplomo*) — only regular (*nova*) and diesel.

If your vehicle needs unleaded gas, write to the EPA in Washington for special permission to have your catalytic converter temporarily removed. Muffler shops will do this only with governmental permission. The cost is about $100. You will need to put the "cat" back in upon your return to the U.S. If you ask the muffler shop to weld flanges to the pipe that will replace the cat, instead of just welding it directly to the exhaust pipe, you will be able to re-install it yourself — as well as be able to remove it again the next time you drive south of the border.

Always carry extra gas with you and top your tank off at every opportunity. Most small towns, like Creel (see Chapter 3), only have one Pemex station. Sometimes they run out of gas for a day or two. Also, buy a bunch of octane enhancer in the U.S. and use some with each tank of Mexican gas. Octane enhancer (*aditivo*) is sold in Mexico, but it is expensive. Gas prices as of November 1988 were 80 cents a gallon.

I recommend only high-clearance vehicles, unless you plan to stick to paved roads. In Copper Canyon Country, this means driving no farther than 40 kilometers past Creel. Four-wheel-drives are necessary in some places and are noted in the appropriate chapters.

One last thing. For years, it was common knowledge that it was a hassle to cross into Mexico because the border officials expected bribes. Then, about ten years ago, the Mexican government, being desirous of American tourists and their dollars, clamped the lid on that. There were wholesale firings of corrupt customs and immigration officials.

Well, that bribery crap might be starting up again. I talked with one party recently who had driven across from El Paso to Juarez. They said the line was four hours long and they had to pay two bribes, totaling $18. I haven't heard anything like this from folks walking across the border.

If you plan on driving down, I suggest you cross over at one of the more isolated border towns: Presidio, Texas/Ojinaga; Columbus, New Mexico/Las Palomas; Douglas, Arizona/Agua Prieta; or Calexico, California/Mexicali.

Getting There

Thousands of people visit Copper Canyon Country every year. More and more are coming all the time. Like most places, the vast majority of these pose little in the way of a tranquility threat to the backcountry user because they never get more than about six feet from the closest road.

There is no way to quantify this, but I would guess that about 95 percent of all visitors to Tarahumara-land arrive via the famed Chihuahua-Pacific train. Almost all of the newspaper and magazine press the Copper Canyon region has received has centered on this train. My favorite line, and I have read this more than once in reputable publications, is that the C-P Railroad runs *through* Copper Canyon. Now, there is no doubt that this railroad is an engineering marvel, but it does *not* go *through* any of the major canyons in Tarahumara-land. From only one spot on the train route, the overlook at El Divisadero, which translated means "overlook," can you even see any part of any of the canyons traditionally lumped into the Las Barrancas del Cobre system. Of course, it is also one of the *best* views you will ever see in your entire life. The train, going both ways, stops at Divisadero for 15 minutes so passengers can hop off to snap a few photos of Urique Canyon, at this point, 1,300 meters deep.

The C-P train route goes from Ojinaga, just across the Rio Grande from Presidio, Texas, to Topolobampo, on the Sea of Cortes. For most Copper Canyon Country visitors, the C-P essentially runs between Chihuahua City and Los Mochis, where it connects with Mexico's major bus, train and plane routes.

The Chihuahua-Pacific covers almost 1,000 kilometers (620 miles) between Ojinaga and Topolobampo. It is joined by three other passenger train routes — the one connecting Juarez/El Paso with Mexico City, the one connecting Nogales with Guadalajara via Mazatlán, and the lesser-known one joining Nuevo Casas Grandes and Cuautemoc. If you are connecting to the Chihuahua-Pacific in Los Mochis and Chihuahua City, each of the lines uses different stations, necessitating taxi rides.

This train ride is among the most beautiful in the world, though in order to appreciate it in world-class terms, you need to board in Los Mochis. If you travel east to west, you pass the most beautiful scenery — between Divisadero and Los Mochis — at night. The scenery between Chihuahua City and Divisadero is nothing to sneeze at, but it's just not quite as splendid.

There are two classes of trains in Mexico, *primero* and *segundo* — first and second. When you buy your ticket (*boleto*) in Los Mochis or Chihuahua City, the ticket agent will automatically assume, if you are a gringo, you want to travel first-class. You probably do, because second-class trains can be quite crowded, real grubby and downright slow. A first-class ticket from Chihuahua City to Creel, the main jumping-off point to Copper Canyon Country, cost about $10 U.S. in November 1988. From Los Mochis to Creel was about $13. It will cost a few dollars more to travel from Chihuahua City to Divisadero, another prime canyon jump-off, two hours west of Creel. Conversely, from Los Mochis to Divisadero will be a few dollars less. Second-class is about a third the cost all the way around.

The first-class trains leave Chihuahua City and Los Mochis at 7:00 a.m., followed an hour later by the second-class train. First-class trains have dining cars. Food vendors — selling everything from sodas and beers to enchiladas and potato chips — usually hop all trains at all stops, so you won't have to starve if you decide to travel second-class. There are no stops along the route of a long enough duration to hop off the train to eat. If you are bypassing Creel in either direction and find yourself in need of basic supplies, there's a small store directly across the tracks from the station.

For more information on the Chihuahua-Pacific Railroad, write to the International Map Company, University of Texas at El Paso, Box 400, El Paso, Texas, 79968-0400. The cost for a nice pamphlet is $2.50.

You can connect directly from the U.S. to Chihuahua City by plane on AeroMexico or Mexicana. Or you can fly to El Paso and hook up with a commuter airline from there to Chihuahua City. Or you can fly to El Paso and cross the border to Juarez. People at the airport will tell you that there's no alternative to the $15 to $20 taxi ride to the border. They lie. If you don't mind walking

Tarahumara girl with her month-old niece near Cusarare.

a few blocks, you can catch the public bus, unless you arrive on a very late flight. Just walk out the main terminal entrance, south to the second traffic light, until you see a bus stop on the right. The bus will take you to the plaza, which is about a mile north of the border. Cost: Under a dollar. (See, I just saved you the cost of this book!)

From Juarez, you can fly, bus or train to Chihuahua City. I recommend the bus, mainly because of the frequency of departures. After passing through immigration, hail a taxi. It will cost about $2 to the bus station. Buses leave to Chihuahua City every half hour or so. First-class busses — those with restrooms — will cost about $10. It's about five hours to Chihuahua.

Trains from Juarez leave at 7:00 a.m., meaning you will have to spend the night in Juarez. The trip to Chihuahua takes about six hours, and you will need to hire a taxi from the border to the train station.

No matter how you arrive, you will want to get to Chihuahua City the night before you plan on hopping the train to Copper Canyon Country. Since there are no hotels near the C-P station, plan on staying at one of the several decent hotels near the bus station. Make arrangements with a taxi driver to come pick you up the next morning in time to get you to the train station. Offer him $5 extra and make certain that the driver understands clearly which train station you want.

If you arrive in Chihuahua City in the middle of the night, which I always seem to do, and you don't want to spend the money on a hotel room for only a few hours, then get a taxi from the bus station directly to the C-P train station. You can just hang out there until morning. I've done this more times than I care to remember. Directly behind the station, on the opposite side from the tracks, there's a little bootleg bar. Ask your taxi driver if he will talk your way in there. It's the only thing near the train station, besides the state prison. Remember: never take your eyes off your gear in this neighborhood. I don't think there's much chance of someone robbing you, but there's always a chance someone could heist your gear.

Busses also connect Chihuahua City with Creel. Inquire at the main bus terminal. Busses take only about three hours, compared to six for the train, but it's nowhere near the experience.

And, don't forget, you can easily drive from Chihuahua City — or from Cuautemoc, if you are coming from the western U.S. — to Copper Canyon Country. It's excellent paved road all the way to Creel with several big towns in between.

There are less options coming from Los Mochis. For one thing, there is no road from there to Tarahumara-land, although one is being built — if the rumors which have persisted for years are true. So, you have no choice but to take the train. Just remember, the C-P train station is half-an-hour by taxi from the city center. So, once again, make arrangements for your taxi ride the night before.

There are several ways to get to Los Mochis. From Nogales, Arizona, you can bus or train, though connections from the rest of the world to Nogales will necessitate a changeover in Tucson. From there, you can take a Greyhound to the border, 60 miles south. I also understand that you can fly from either Tucson or Nogales to Los Mochis. You can also catch a ferry from La Paz, on the Baja, to Topolobampo. From there, it's only a few minutes by bus to Los Mochis.

If you are coming from southern Mexico, connections to both Los Mochis and Chihuahua City will be very easy, whether you travel by plane, train, bus or car. Basically, if you want to get to

Chihuahua City, start in Mexico City. If you want to get to Los Mochis, start in Guadalajara.

On your way home, plan on spending a day in either Los Mochis or Chihuahua City. Though neither is your classic tourist destination, they are each very interesting. I especially like Chihuahua City. Check the bibliography for *South America on a Shoestring*, which includes Mexico, for some specifics about these cities.

Languages

Spanish and Tarahumara. Don't expect to find much English once you get to Copper Canyon Country. A few of the employees at some of the lodging facilities in the area — the Parador de la Montaña in Creel, Las Cabañas del Cobre in Cusarare, the Hotel Divisadero de las Barrancas in Divisadero and Bustillo's in Batopilas, among maybe one or two others — speak varying amounts of English. Once you head out into the backcountry, expect to rely totally on Español.

No one should bypass a trip to Mexico because they don't speak a lick of Spanish. Though, of course, the more you can learn before you head south of the border, the better. With less than six months of diligent study, you will not only be able to order a beer properly, but at the same time, you will be making a cultural statement to the locals. Americans are perceived, rightly or wrongly, as being linguistically arrogant. A little Spanish will go a long way towards modifying that perception.

And, besides, Mexicans are the antitheses of Parisians. They are the most patient and helpful people in the world when it comes to learning their language. They are extremely flattered that you are making the effort. They praise your attempts mightily. And, if it becomes necessary, they will usually correct your foul-ups very gently. It's a great scene.

Most Tarahumara men speak Spanish, though it is their second language. So you'll be on equal footing. Tarahumara woman, especially the older ones, may only speak Tarahumara, although this is almost inconsequential because they're generally too shy to speak to strangers.

I have tried repeatedly to bone up on my Tarahumara. Lost

cause. My tongue, lips and larynx will not physiologically do some of the things required to get even the most basic Tara words out. And the mainframe of my brain will not make enough room for the words. They visit, and they move on.

If you find yourself in the company of Tarahumaras, by all means ask them to teach you a few words and phrases. They get a little shy about this sometimes, but they seem to think it's amusing to listen to gringos mispronouncing their babble.

You'll point to the fire and ask, *"Como se llama?"* — how is this called — while pointing to the flames. They'll smile coyly and, very softly, say *"Ickwiiijzjzjwak"* — mixed with several guttural embellishments. You will attempt to repeat the word, and all the Taras present will giggle at you.

The Tarahumara Mission Store in Creel sells a Spanish-Tara dictionary and the map that Dr. Schmidt sells contains a small English-Spanish-Tara glossary.

A few backpacking words to add to your list:

English	**Español**
to hike	camionar
to camp	acampar
trail	camino or sendero
How far is it to...?	Cuando hay de aqui al...?
highway	carretera
pavement	pavimento
far	lejo
very far	muy lejo
close	cerca
very close	cerquita
boot	bota
backpacker	mochilero (a)
backpack	mochila
white gas	gasolina blanca
kerosene	keroseno
backpacking stove	estufa de acampar
sleeping bag	bolsa de dormiendo
tent	casita de acampar
guide	guia
map	mapa

cold beer	cerveza fria
rum	ron
cigars	cigarros puros
Fill 'er up.	Lleno.

One last note about languages. Don't worry about messing up. Everyone does it. Some people even go so far as to say that you can't get on with the business of learning a second language until you've embarrassed yourself major league at least once.

There was the time a buddy of mine ordered a *perro caliente* — a hot dog, he thought — from a street vendor. Everyone for nine blocks was immediately rolling on the ground with laughter. Come to find out the Spanish term for hot dog is *jot dog*, pronounced exactly as it is pronounced in English. *Perro caliente* means "bitch in heat."

My buddy didn't even bat an eye. He just continued his quest to become bilingual, secure in the knowledge that he had already screwed up as badly as a person could possibly screw up without getting locked up.

The Tarahumaras

We don't call Copper Canyon Country "Tarahumara-land" for nothing. This area is the home field for the world-famous, long-distance-running Tarahumara Indians. The Tarahumaras — Taras, for short — are the second largest North American Indian tribe after the Navajos. Best guesstimates put their numbers at about 50,000.

When you visit Copper Canyon Country, it is nearly the same as entering an American Indian Reservation, although the legal set-up is more fragmented. You must consider your every move in terms of how it will likely impact the Taras. This is their land and "we" have no right to be there, except the right that they give us.

The Taras migrated to Copper Canyon Country from the high plains around modern-day Cuautemoc about 500 years ago, after the Spanish Conquistadores started enslaving them to work the local silver mines. It wasn't a mass migration in the exodus sense, but, rather, a very gradual process that took place family by family. As households got fed up with having their children enslaved, they moved west, into the canyon country. The Conquistadores sometimes gave chase, only to find themselves looking down into the majestic depths of Copper Canyon. This, they decided, was simply not worth it. So, the Taras, were pretty much left alone.

After a while, the descendants of those Conquistadores who stayed in Mexico began settling on the edges of Tarahumara-land. Afterall, there was lots of stuff they wanted — silver, gold, timber and land.

The Taras have lived on the fringes of the Mexican-run extractive industries ever since, interacting with it sometimes, ignoring it, and being ignored by it, at other times.

The Taras have been known to get riled and come out of the woodwork. During the Mexican Revolution of 1910-19, both sides signed an agreement that battles would no longer be fought in Tarahumara-land. Seems the peace and tranquility of the Taras' scene was threatened by the fighting. To demonstrate the depth of their irritation, the Taras would frequently sneak into whichever side's camp was handiest — the Taras didn't give a hoot in hell who was in power in Mexico City — and drench the slumbering soldiers with gasoline and set them on fire. Full-body hot-foots.

The Taras wanted nothing more than to be left alone. This, my friends, is the best way to characterize the Tarahumaras and their culture. When you see where some Tarahumara families live, you will be convinced. *They just want to be left alone.*

Taras are, towards outsiders, very aloof, standoffish and shy. This is not to say that they aren't basically friendly people. Neither is it to say that many Taras aren't very gregarious. Some are. Many are not.

It *is* to say that you should always assume, until provided ample reason to believe otherwise, that the Taras' privacy is sacrosanct. They cruise through life with a privacy force-field around them and around their property.

I don't know that Taras have developed culture-wide feelings about whether gringos are "good" or "bad." Our "invasion" of their turf is still too new. I do know that they have made judgments about some of our peculiar ways. Some good. Some bad.

So, we are at the fragile point in the meeting of cultures where "we" — Americans, gringos, tourists, backpackers — can make a good impression for a change. Here are some things.

If there's any way to avoid it, you should never pass onto a Tara's land uninvited. Tara dwellings do not end at the front door. They end at the fence surrounding their land. When you walk up to a Tara's house without being asked to do so, it's the same as someone walking up to the foot of your bed without your permission. (Thanks to Skip McWilliams for that phrasing.)

If you want to talk with Taras — to ask directions, for instance — the mannerly thing to do is to sit outside their property fence and wait. If they want to talk, they will come to you. Eventually.

Never photograph Taras without asking their permission. Most Taras will tell you, politely but firmly, that they would rather not be photographed. Certainly, this is their right.

You should also be very careful about taking photos of Tara dwellings. Taras consider their houses and their land to be extensions of themselves. So, if you photograph their *casita*, you are, at the same time, taking a picture of them. Again, you can ask, but, if they say no, don't try to talk them into it. And certainly don't try to bribe them. This is justifiably insulting and speaks poorly of our culture. You can offer a tip after you take your shots. This you should do respectfully, making certain that they know that you know that they have done you the favor, not the other way around simply because some cash changed hands.

As well, there are plenty of old missions located in Tarahumaraland. The Taras are all basically Catholic, though many are far less Catholic than they let on to be. They take their missions very seriously. You are generally welcome to walk around inside. Remove your hat. And leave a small offering, perhaps 100 pesos, on the altar.

And, unlike a few places I know, it is considered very bad form to offer to buy the children.

When you are hiking in the backcountry, you may find yourself on a collision course with a herd of goats. If there's any way to do so, try to not disrupt the proceedings. Tara goats are used to people. So, if you just stand still, they will pass around you with no problem. If the herd spooks, some poor Tara girl will have to, with the aid of her dogs, run up and down steep hills until she rounds the herd up.

Also — and please forgive me if this sounds overly didactic in tone — you may stumble across Tara artifacts, especially pots, in the outback. As tempting as it may be, these should be admired, photographed and otherwise left alone.

The Taras are some seriously primitive people. They are often referred to as "genuine cave dwellers" in the prints, in a tone that borders on "ain't that precious." There are plenty of Taras who do, indeed, dwell in caves, though a small percentage of the population. And they *are* precious.

The Taras are semi-nomadic people. Tara families will have as many as five residences. One might be located near the place they grow beans. Another next to some good goat-grazing territory. Each of the places has a specific use.

The Taras are also near-puritanical in their day-to-day life. You don't, for instance, want to skinny dip in front of a Tara homestead. They dress modestly and it is polite for you to do the same in their presence.

The one exception to this shy, puritanical attitude is when the Taras commence to drinking. I have read that the Taras are drunk most of the time. This is simply not the case.

The Taras drink mainly during ceremonial occasions called *tesguinadas*. During *tesguinadas*, which usually last three or four days and are by invitation only, Taras consume vast amounts of *tesguino* — corn beer ingloriously described by Skip McWilliams as tasting like spiked creamed corn mixed with a bushel of grass clippings.

During *tesguinadas*, most anything goes, especially if it has to do with spousal-exchange programs. When the festivities are over — meaning when all the corn beer is gone — the Taras dust themselves off and stumble back to the straight and narrow.

During the winter, the Tara men, with little else to do, spend more time drinking in non-*tesguinada* environments. Tequila is the beverage of choice. And they drink a lot of tequila when the chance presents itself. Say it I must — the Taras make for some seriously nasty drunks. They may be fun to each other, but they are certainly not fun to gringos, even if the gringos are equally as drunk. It's best to avoid such situations.

Otherwise, you will likely have no problems with the Taras.

They are kind and gentle people and I get to like them more every time I visit Copper Canyon Country.

Management

Almost all the land in Copper Canyon Country is part of Mexico's *ejido* system, established by Pancho Villa after he and his followers won the Mexican Revolution. Villa sent representatives into the countryside who gave communal title to land traditionally occupied by the local indigenous population. This is one of the most-noteworthy land reform programs ever initiated in the history of the world.

This is where Tara "reservations" differ from American Indian Reservations. Title was given on a village-by-village basis, rather than on a tribal basis. Therefore, though the cumulative acreage of all the *ejidos* in Tarahumara-land would make for a good-sized chunk of land, it is broken down into communally owned smaller parcels, each of which is governed by an elected council, which may or may not be the real local power center. Some *ejidos* put more stock in their traditional chief concept.

You enter an *ejido* by the grace of the people of that *ejido*. And you enter the next *ejido* by the grace of the people of *that ejido*. No sort of permit system has been established, though that may be forthcoming in the next decade.

It is a mannerly thing, when camping near a *ranchito*, to let someone know what you're up to and, out of courtesy, ask for permission. If there is a mission nearby, make a small donation. Never camp on fenced property without permission, and always offer to pay a few hundred pesos for the privilege. By the way, there are no signs welcoming you to whatever *ejido* it is you're about to enter. And they're not marked on maps.

Money

Mexican peso. In late-December 1988, the peso was valued at about 2,260 to one U.S. dollar. There were rumors circulating at the time that it was about to be devalued to around 5,000 to one. Because of future uncertainty, I give most cost information in U.S. dollars.

The Mexican government allows businesses to change dollars into pesos and vice-versa. Usually, your best rate of exchange will be at a bank, because there is no black market for currency. Banks will usually charge some kind of commission.

If you can't find a bank, look for a *casa del cambio*. Your rate won't be as good as the bank, but you usually won't be charged a commission. Rates can be slightly lower for travelers checks (TCs) than for cash.

If all else fails, walk into a grocery store and ask if they buy dollars. If you have cash, this will be very easy. With TCs it can be more of a hassle, but certainly not impossible. Many places will want to look at your passport when changing TCs.

Of course, you will lose money when you want to change pesos to dollars, so try to time it so you run out of pesos the same time you're leaving the country.

Personal checks are generally a no go. Credit cards are accepted by many larger hotels, stores and restaurants in the bigger cities. But, once you get off the beaten path, you'll have little luck with plastic. Carry small denominations of currency. Small change is often in short supply in the boonies.

Staying Healthy, Including Water Purification

You don't need any shots to visit Mexico, though there are those who would recommend getting a gamma globulin shot for infectious (type-A) hepatitis. This shot, which you can save yourself some bucks by getting at a public health facility rather than a private doctor's office, leaves you stiff-hammed for a few days. Nobody says it is perfectly effective, and it only lasts about six weeks.

Hepatitis is probably the biggest health concern for Copper Canyon Country, except for falling off a cliff. Type-A is spread through contaminated water, or by eating food handled by a carrier or someone who has come in contact with contaminated water. The best prevention is to consume only purified water and eat raw fruits and vegetables only when peeled by you and rinsed with purified water.

Many people will avoid eating salads. If you're only going to be in Mexico for a week, maybe that's not a bad idea. But, if you're there for a longer period of time, it will start having serious health implications if you avoid salads entirely. You'll just have to take more chances than you would like. I have just said to hell with it. I eat anything in Mexico and have had nothing worse than constipation. My time is coming, though, and I know it.

When purifying water, remember, hepatitis is viral. You cannot rely on your backpacking water pump. The only one with any pretension whatsoever of taking care of hep-virus is the $200 Swiss-made Katadyn. This is, by far, the best backpacking water filter on the market. I carry one, and I have also used a First Need, which, though much cheaper and somewhat lighter, is nowhere near as thorough, and is much more inconvenient in the long-run. The First Need has a disposable filter element that, once clogged, is useless. I have had a couple First Need filters clog up on me, under admittedly extreme circumstances, but circumstances, nonetheless, that I found myself in need of clean water — after only a few uses. You can back-flush the filter to prolong its life, but once it is clogged, it's history.

The Katadyn utilizes a filter that is ultimately disposable, in that it reaches a point where it no longer works and, therefore, needs to be tossed and replaced. It's just that it can be used over three years in the worst situations imaginable on a day-to-day basis before its days are done.

The ceramic filter unscrews from the pump mechanism. All you do is clean the filter with a brush that comes with the unit and re-assemble the housing. You're back in business.

Herb Koelble, who is head of Katadyn's American distribution center, told me that his filter is able to take care of stuff down to .2 microns in size. Viruses are way smaller than that. But, Koelble says, viruses generally hook up with something a little larger, like a bacteria or amoeba — both of which are larger than .2 microns. Therefore, the Katadyn takes care of things.

Even for those viruses that prefer to cruise unattended, the way is not smooth because the Katadyn's filter pores are zig-zag-shaped. So, the virus can get caught up before it hits your water bottle. Then, it will perish because the filter is impregnated with some silver stuff that apparently spells doom for viruses.

But this, again, is no guarantee. So, Koelble suggests, if you are in an area known to have viral contamination lurking about

— and this information can be found from a call to the U.S. State Department — that you add about a half a dose of iodine-based tablets, sold in outdoor stores with the brand-name "Potable Agua," *after* filtering it. He says that iodine latches onto the murk in murky water as enthusiastically as it latches onto little goobers that carry disease. Iodine is not intelligent life. So, the more muck you remove from the water, the less confusion factor for the iodine molecules.

Just remember, though you can get away by using a lot less iodine after filtration, you still need to let it work for however long it says on the bottle. If you have no filter, you will have to rely solely on either iodination or boiling.

Either way, bear in mind that this is hot territory. You will have to suck down lots of water. Iodine is not meant to be consumed in large amounts for long periods of time. So, try to rely on boiling as much as possible. Whatever you do, don't go thirsty because it is a hassle to purify water.

There is a chance you might catch a case of the runs. This is almost always caused by the introduction of regional-dwelling bacteria into the ol' intestines. It will take about three days for your system to get used to the local micro-critters, which can jump into your here and now via food, water, soft drinks, whatever. This doesn't imply that a given country is un-clean. Mexicans likewise get Uncle Sam's revenge when they're visiting the States. It's just a matter of what your system's used to.

Should you find yourself going through toilet paper at a major rate, just make sure that you keep drinking plenty of water. Dehydration is not good. It is generally considered preferable to avoid anti-diarrhea medicine, unless things get way out of hand. If you suspect you only have Montezuma's revenge, you should let the beast pass from your bowels.

Dysentery, in both amoebic and bacillary forms, is also a concern, but, by taking the same precautions you are taking to prevent hepatitis, you should have no problem with it. You will need some medications you probably won't have in your first aid kit to take care of amoebic dysentery. So, if you notice blood and/or mucus in your stool, you might want to seek medical care.

A surprising number of people suffer from constipation when traveling. As hard as it may seem since raw fruits and veggies

Tarahumara grain storage building above Tararecua Canyon.

are suspect, you need to keep up your roughage intake while on the road. Buy fruits and veggies from food stores and cleanse them yourself. Don't eat too much white flour and lay off the Mennonite cheese if things start clogging up.

You will also want to read up on heat exhaustion — a type of shock caused by the body's attempts to cool itself — and heat stroke — when the body's internal thermostat goes on the blink. Check out the book, *Wilderness Medicine*, listed in the bibliography.

One more thing. The most common cause of pre-mature death among the Tarahumaras is tuberculosis. I heard a second-hand story, wherein the person telling me this had been told by a public health nurse that in 20-some-odd years of working with the Tarahumaras, *everyone* she had tested was a TB carrier.

The temptation would be to recommend that you not participate in any passing-of-the-bottle-around-the-campfire or passing-of-the-cigar rituals. But, in addition to that being somewhat socially awkward at times, it would also deprive you of some good experiences. I have seen Taras wipe the mouth of the bottle after having it passed to them, so it is socially acceptable to do the same, though it will probably be a waste of time if any TB slime is on the bottle. If you do notice a Tara coughing a lot, I would avoid sharing a water or tequila bottle with him — the stuff that they cough up being the point of concern.

Other than that, travel in this part of Mexico with no more caution that you would travel in your own country.

Staying Alive

There are some critters and plants around here that could prove inconvenient. Just about every group will have at least one member who will have an encounter with a rattlesnake. One member of my party once had a three-foot rattler just about crawl directly into her lap while we were sitting around the campfire one night. Another person I know found himself sitting next to a six-foot rattler.

The good thing about rattlers, as opposed to some of the other more slimy, nightmarish species like mambas and vine snakes, is that they *rattle*. You wouldn't believe what an effective reflexive deterrent rattling can be to progressing any further with the physical act you are currently engaged in. You don't even have to think about it. The deep recesses of your evasive action control have matters well in hand before you even know what's going on.

Rattlers are, despite their fierce, macho image, a very weenie species — maybe even the biggest weenie reptile species in the world. Lower than box turtles. I mean, what other intensely fearsome critter has evolved a *body part* that amounts to nothing more than a purely audible version of a human wetting in his or her pants from fright?

A rattler, when rattling, is pleading for mercy — telling you in no uncertain terms that it doesn't mind one bit being branded the most-cowardly creature in the canyon. Yes, give a rattler the chance to high-tail it, so to speak, in the opposite direction, and it will take it.

You just need to make certain you give it the chance to do just that. If you get too close or touch it, you are going to get bit. And, even though envenomation fails to transpire about a fourth of the time, those aren't my kind of odds.

So, don't put your appendages anywhere you can't see. That simple precaution will all but totally ensure that you will not suffer snakebite — unless, of course, one crawls into your lap while you're sitting around the campfire.

There are also coral snakes in Copper Canyon Country, just like the American southwest. I have never heard of anyone even seeing one.

Either way, I suggest you read *Wilderness Medicine* before entering the backcountry. It goes into some detail on snakebite.

There are poisonous spiders around — black widows, tarantulas and maybe brown recluses. Another local funlover is called an "assassin bug." I kid you not. *Wilderness Medicine*, likewise, goes into detail about this little critter. Many people feel a lot more comfortable sleeping in a tent when in the deep canyons, where more of this poisonous stuff lives.

And Copper Canyon Country is home to lots of cactus. As well as mesquite groves. Bushwhacking can sometimes require blood transfusions. For those of you allergic to poison ivy, there is some in the deep canyons.

But that's about it. No more bad stuff than the Carolinas. And probably even less.

Maps

There are two topographical series, the 1:250,000-scale "San Juanito" map and roughly six to eight — depending on where you draw the boundaries of Copper Canyon Country — 1:50,000-scale maps. I list the appropriate maps in the "Particulars" section of each chapter. Remember that these maps will be in kilometers and the contour intervals in meters. (One mile equals about 1.6 kilometers and one foot equals about .3 meters; or, one kilometer equals .6 miles and one meter equals 3.3 feet.)

These maps are geo-physically accurate, as far as I can tell. The topographic data undoubtedly came straight from U.S. satellites. But the trail and town data is often way off. Do not rely too heavily on trail markings on the maps. Become familiar with the landmarks in your area and then look, on the ground, rather than on the map, for your trail. Also, many of the *ranchitos* marked on the maps are in the wrong place. Some by a long distance. Sitagochi comes to mind.

All maps of the area, with the exception of the map covering Basaseachi Falls, are sold at the Tarahumara Mission Store in

Creel. I have yet to hear of a successful attempt to purchase these maps in advance through the mail.

A Note On Place Name Spellings

It is common for the little backcountry dots on your Tarahumara-land maps to end in "chi." Pamachi. Tehuirichi. Panalachi. Sitagochi. I guess this means "ville" or something. You may also see, or hear, these names with a "c" tacked on. Pamachic. Panalachic. Don't be confused. The "c" ending is just a slight Spanish-ization of these Tara place-names. Basaseachi is the same place as Basaseachic.

Guides

Though I am hardly an expert on the subject of guided trips, I still, somewhat old fashionedly I'm afraid, feel that trip planning and preparation are an important part of the wilderness travel process. By studying the maps for hundreds of hours and packaging your own food back in the bleakness of civilization, you are establishing an important pre-trip bond with the place you are heading to. That, I believe, causes you to arrive on the scene more mentally prepared for the trip.

As well, and again, I know how 1950s-Boy-Scout-like this sounds, I think there's a higher level of post-trip gratification if you and your buddies pulled the trip off without professional help.

I understand that many people disagree with me on this, or at least don't agree to the extent that they're foregoing any guided trip as a result. I just want you to understand that Copper Canyon Country is very available to you if you have any semblance of trip-planning ability.

If you decide, for whatever reason, that you'd prefer visiting the area with a guide, here are a couple of suggestions:

Skip McWilliams
% Las Cabañas del Cobre
1103 E. Big Beaver
Troy, Michigan 48084
(800) 521-1455
(Specializes in trips for beginners)

American Wilderness Experience
P. O. Box 1486
Boulder, Colorado 80306
(303) 444-2632

Sunracer Tours
P. O. Box 40092
Tucson, AZ 85717
(602) 881-0243

There are also other guides operating in Copper Canyon Country, some of whom are surely very good.

While in Copper Canyon Country, you may wish to hire a Tarahumara guide, for your whole trip or just one segment. Understand before you do so that these people have no great tradition of embarking on wilderness forays with relatively affluent gringos, like the Sherpas. They don't always manage to figure out what it is you want of them. And I don't know if many Taras have it figured out why we are there. I've asked several if they know why we pay them to take us out into the boondocks, just so we can come back three days later.

The response has amounted to massive shoulder-shrugging.

You need to let your Tara guide know that you want to take the best trail, rather than the most direct trail. *No queremos un camino feo. Queremos un camino mas facil* ("We don't want an ugly trail. We want an easier trail.") should do the trick, although you may have to repeat yourself more than once during the trip.

You must also ask them to lead you at a slower pace, because the Taras flat out fly on the trail. If you try to keep up with them, you're doomed. *Ande mas despacio* — "walk slower" — and *nos espera* — "wait for us" — should work. Also, remind your guide to let you know if you pass near anything interesting, like abandoned mine shafts or a spring.

You will be able to hire a Tara guide by just asking around in Divisadero, Cusarare or Creel. Expect to pay about $5 a day, with you supplying the food. You need to know some things about this food part.

One of the main reasons Taras hire out as guides — and many do not — is because they are interested in checking us out. They are especially interested in our food. Taras have some proud appetites. They will eat every item they can get their hands on. I have witnessed a group of Tara guides threaten to quit a trip if the food offerings did not improve. This despite the fact that the reason the food situation was not up to stuff was because these same Taras had been eating everything in sight for the last three days.

Once when dividing up supplies, I stupidly had my Tara guide carry the lunches and snacks. Two days later, we realized that he had been hiking up ahead and diving into the food bag. With two days left in our trip, we found ourselves going without lunch food.

So, you've got to establish a workable food disbursement plan. Before the trip gets underway, lay the food out in front of your guide. Make certain that he understands that what he sees before him is the total food supply. Ask him if he thinks it's enough and if there's anything else he can think of that you might need. Tell him what your basic chronological meal consumption habits are. Point out that you will stop for several snacks per day on the trail, for instance. This way, if any problems do arise on the trail, you can refer back to this conversation.

If you pass around a bag of candy, the best procedure is to either say how many pieces each person gets, or to just hand over the correct number. This goes for serving supper out of a communal pan. You need to make your guide understand that you are on relatively limited rations; that you, as a group, can only eat certain amounts of certain foods at certain times. This should cause no friction, as long as the rations are interesting and reasonably ample. If they are not, you may lose your guide mid-trip.

You will also be expected to buy your guide cigarettes. He will be responsible for his own blanket. You will likely have to dig up a cheap bowl, spoon and cup — easily accomplished along the main drag in Creel.

If, before leaving home, you are certain that you are going to hire a Tara guide, you may want to bring an extra pack and sleeping pad. Whatever guide you eventually hire would be mighty pleased to have use of them. Just make certain he understands that it's a loan — *un prestamo*. And, if for whatever reason you don't end up hiring a guide, you can just ask the proprietors of whichever lodging facility you stay at in Creel to hold onto the extra gear while you're in the backcountry.

Several of the lodging facilities provide guide services. Most have a set price, regardless of the number of customers, up to the point that there's no more room in the vehicle. Whenever one of the hikes described in this book can be accessed by a tour out of Creel, I make mention of that fact.

Gifts

This is something you might give some thought to before leaving home. It is tradition with American travelers that we go out and buy balloons or jellybeans or sewing needles or cigars or costume jewelry to give away to locals we meet on the trail. As well, many people decide to lay gifts or tips on their guide after the trip.

Some places have well-established guidelines for gift and tip giving. Since Copper Canyon Country is new to this game, it does not. Therefore, "we" have the opportunity to establish some sane ground rules. Unfortunately, I have no definite ideas on what those ground rules should be.

I am tempted to suggest that candy not be given, for health reasons, mainly. But, hell, what harm's a few peanut M&Ms going to do to a Tara who will never visit a dentist his entire life and gets sweets maybe twice a year? If some Tara children hang around my camp, I can't resist giving them a cookie or some candy. You almost feel like Santa Claus if you pass something out.

At the same time, it would be a drag if the Taras got to expecting handfuls of goodies every time a gringo passed by. The children in some of the Mexican villages around Batopilas are already doing this — running out in droves and asking if you could spare some *dulces* — candies — as you pass by.

With the Taras, this is not too far-fetched. I have seen Americans who have brought full *bags* of trinkets, baubles and curiosities, with the intention of just handing it all out. This only encourages outright begging, which seems to be on the increase as well, though we're still talking small potatoes compared to urban Mexico.

I guess the only thing to do is stick to your personal beliefs about gifts. If it makes you feel good at whatever level, do it. If it makes you feel as though you are aiding and abetting the corruption of a pure society, don't.

At the trinket level, costume jewelry, candy, tobacco products, sewing supplies and brightly colored cloth are popular.

You may want to give someone — perhaps your guide — something more substantial than a trinket or candy. Things that any Tara family would appreciate include good quality knives, axes and clothes.

Physical Preparation

We both know I have to write this part and we both know you have to read it. At the same time, we both know that it will likely not induce you to get in shape before coming to Copper Canyon Country, any more than it will induce me. We'll both continue to practice those 12-ounce curls right up until the day we leave for Mexico. But, let's go through the motions.

Hiking around Tarahumara-land is physically demanding — all the more so because it can get unbelievably hot. Multi-hour steep ups and downs are hard on the legs, especially the feet, thighs, knees, calves, ankles, shins, Achilles tendons and toes.

You are well advised to embark on a fitness/diet regimen at least a couple of months before your visit. Steve Ilg's book, *The Outdoor Athlete, Total Training for Outdoor Performance*, listed in the bibliography, is the best I have seen for getting backpackers in shape. Or, at least for making us feel guilty about the fact that we've blown it off again.

Seasons

For deep canyon trips, dead winter is best. The deep canyons are too hot except from late-November to early-March. Even as early as mid-March, the daytime highs regularly exceed 100 degrees F. Nighttime lows in the winter necessitate three-season bags only. As well, the black flies get bad towards summer. Avoid the rainy season, mid-July to mid-September, because of the flash flood danger. Best time for photography is just after the rainy season ends. From that point until the rains return next summer, things get browner and browner. For trips in the mountains, just about any time of year is good.

I personally prefer the end of the rainy season, because the rivers are warm enough to swim in very comfortably — especially if they are near any hot springs (*aguascalientes*).

Nighttime lows in the dead of winter in the high country will always be below freezing. It can easily get below zero at night. And it can snow. Daytime highs are usually in the sun-drenched 60s or 70s F. Come prepared for the extremes.

Fires

There's plenty of driftwood along the rivers in the deep canyons. In such locations, building fires is probably okay. Away from the rivers, you're going to have to make a judgement call. It can be argued that the thin dry soil is extremely reliant on the organic matter from felled trees and branches. At the same time, the Taras rely on the local wood for survival. So, it would probably be better if you used a stove.

If you are camping with any Taras, though, you'll have a fire regardless of what you may think of the matter. A Tarahumara would look at you very funny if you told them they ought not build a fire there in the middle of Tarahumara-land. These people are fire magicians. They revere flames. They love sleeping with their heads near 'bouts in the coals.

You may be able to convince them that it's more practical to cook on a stove, but they will be listening to your arguments while cozying up to the fire they have just built.

Wildlife

While Copper Canyon Country is geo-physically and culturally as wonderful as any place on the continent, alas, when it comes to wildlife viewing, it is no Yellowstone.

I have seen a huge flock of parrots, a few snakes, a few squirrels, a coati, a raccoon and herds of goats, cows and chickens. Besides lizards, that's about all you're likely to see. Animals are very wary in Copper Canyon Country. Tarahumaras will attempt to kill and eat just about anything with a heartbeat. You may lay eyes on fox, wild turkey, eagle, mule deer, bighorn sheep, mountain lion, jaguar, peccary or, if your karmic affairs are in very good order, a Mexican wolf or a grizzly. The latter two may be extinct in Tarahumara-land, but who knows?

Gear

For average backpacking trips of less than a week's duration in Copper Canyon Country, you don't need to run out and buy thousands of dollars worth of new gear. At the same time, you don't want your gear falling apart on you at the bottom of Sinforosa Canyon. Focus most of your attention on footwear. After that, in descending order of importance, come water purification system, pack, sleeping bag, tent, raingear, stove.

Once you determine what time of year you will be coming to Tarahumara-land, and whether or not you will be heading into the deep canyons, you can draw on your own experience as to what you'll need.

Some specific recommendations:

Hat. Get a good one that will keep your face from getting sizzled; the sun in this area can be intense.

Sunglasses. Same thing; get good ones with UV protection.

Backpack. I recommend a medium-sized (4,500 to 5,000 cubic inch capacity) internal-frame pack — preferably one that is no wider than your body and no taller than your head. The latter of primary concern if you end up doing any bushwhacking. That said, I have been using a new Lowe Frame Pack Deluxe, with a capacity of about 6,100 cubic inches — mainly because I am overloaded with camera gear. My wife carries a Mountainsmith Frostfire II. She loves it.

Raingear. We usually just carry a Gore-tex shell. No rain pants.

Sleeping Bag. For winter camping in the high country, you need a bag rated to at least five-below. For winter camping in the deep canyons, a 45-degree rating should do it. For summer camping in the high country, a 40-degree rating will be sufficient. All non-winter camping in the deep canyons requires nothing more than a fiber-pile tropical bag or a bedsheet.

Sleeping Pad. This is desert country with lots of stickery plants. Be careful with your self-inflating pad. Always lay it on a groundcloth and keep it inside your pack when hiking.

Boots. Make sure you have good boots in good condition. I once had a pair of soft boots blow out on me in the worst possible situation in Tararecua Canyon. My back-up shoes were some cheap running jobbies with badly worn tread. I don't want to go through that again, and neither do you. You can do worse than using new, soft boots, like Hi-Techs. The problem with soft boots is that people believe they do all the same things as sturdier, mid-weight boots, but that they just wear out faster. False. They do not provide the same amount of support, especially on rough trails with heavy weight. Very light, soft boots are made for on-trail day hiking. If you use them in Copper Canyon Country, especially on the steep downhill grades, with a week's worth of food in your pack, you are probably going to suffer from very sore feet. I recommend mid-weight books, like the Asolo Super Scouts. They cost more — almost $120 at last look — but they will last a lot longer and they will be much easier on your feet.

Back-Up Shoes. Don't overlook this. I always recommend that people bring camp shoes that they can hike in, in case there are problems with their boots. Trail shoes, such as the Nike Son of Lava Dome, would fit the bill nicely, though they are a little on the heavy side. New running shoes, with knobby tread, will do just fine. These you will wear for river crossings. Teva sandals are okay, but about dusk in the deep canyons, the biting flies can be bad. And, as we all know, biting flies love ankles.

Tent. In the high country, the frost can be intense in the winter. I always use a tent then. I never use one in the canyons. I bring a groundcloth and a tent fly, in the unlikely event of rain. Because of snakes, scorpions and assassin bugs, you may feel more comfortable in a tent, even though the temperature and precipitation concerns do not merit carrying one. Go with something very light-weight. Afterall, you are not likely to be tent-bound for three days in Tarahumara-land. You won't need a vestibule. I've been impressed recently with The North Face Tadpole for deep canyon trips, though it isn't appropriate for the high country in winter, unless you carry a really warm bag.

Water Purification. See section in this chapter sub-titled "Staying Healthy."

Water Bottles. Carry at least two liters worth of water bottles. Hikes out of the deep canyons can take most of the day. You may walk for hours on end with no shade, in direct sunlight, with temperatures well over 100 degrees F. I always carry a three-gallon water bag for camp use.

First Aid Kit. Carry as much of one as you can. See *Wilderness Medicine* for specific recommendations.

Just remember the old sailor's adage: "Go cheap, go light, and go NOW!" Don't get overly caught up in gear acquisition. You can hike in Tarahumara-land with your old Kelty Tioga. Iodine will do if you don't have a water filter. You don't need to buy a bunch of new stuff, unless you are looking to upgrade your gear anyhow.

The Jesuits

The Jesuits are a very powerful political, as well as spiritual, force in Tarahumara-land. They have been in these parts for a long time, they speak Tarahumara, and they have a death grip on Tara salvation. The Taras take the Jesuits very seriously and they fear them. Most Taras who have had any formal education at all, studied under the Jesuits. And, for the last decade or so, they have been taught in Tarahumara. The Jesuits role in your visit will probably be minimal, but don't underestimate their influence with the Taras. I'll be offering some insights into this important aspect of Tara life throughout the book.

Some Final Observations

Tarahumara Ranchitos. You will notice lots of dots on your maps with place-names. Do not assume these are little towns. They are, for the most part, *ranchitos* — little Tara settlements with usually no more than a handful of dwellings. Do not count on buying anything at a *ranchito*. This is not to say that you might not be able to buy a little food, if you really need it and they really have it. But don't plan on it. A couple of the small Mexican outback villages have very tiny stores selling soft drinks, crackers and sardines.

Thievery. I have near-perfect confidence in the honesty of the Tarahumaras. You want to be careful in and around Mexican settlements, but no more so than around rural settlements in the U.S.

Rainy Season. Between about mid-July and mid-September, it rains a lot, usually in the form of late afternoon cloudbursts. In addition to watching your rear for lightning in the high country, keep a lookout for high water in the canyons — even very small ones. During rainy season, river levels are *much* higher on a day-to-day basis. You will not be able to cross the Urique below Divisadero, for instance, until several weeks after rainy season ends. At the same time, flash floods are the most-powerful natural phenomenon in Tarahumara-land. A bone dry, fairly small *arroyo* can suddenly became a major-league torrent with little notice. It doesn't even have to be raining or even cloudy where you are. As long as it's raining up-canyon from you, you're in danger. Never camp in canyon bottoms, no matter how small, no matter how dry, during rainy season. I have lived for more than a decade in flash-flood territory, and I have seen unbelievable damage caused by seemingly innocuous little creeks. Likewise, just because a river, like the Urique, is flowing fast and strong in flood stage, doesn't mean that it is immune from relative flash flooding. Water levels, even those that are already very high, can rise very quickly. And very fatally. Please take this seriously.

Drugs. In some places in Copper Canyon Country, especially around Batopilas, this can be a serious situation. But, if you act intelligently, you will have no problems. The main drug of concern in Tarahumara-land is marijuana, though none is cultivated, that I have seen, near any of the route itineraries I have described in this guide. The people who grow this weed, if the tales be true, all lack senses of humor. They carry weapons and I have no doubt they will use them under the right circumstances.

Should you find yourself in the midst of a pot field, you need to act NOW. This is not the time to thank Buddha for your good fortune, while setting up camp with one hand and stuffing sticky buds into your pocket with the other. You need to leave the area immediately. Retrace your footsteps, no matter the inconvenience factor. If you are confronted, play stupid. They will likely suspect you of being a Yanqui Fed. You need to convince them otherwise. If you succeed in convincing them that you are nothing more than a disoriented tourist, who has NOT SEEN *anything* suspicious and who would not know it if he had, then you will likely just be escorted away rather briskly.

The military presence is strong in this area, especially on the road between Creel and Batopilas. I have talked to many people, some so straight-looking that you can't help but giggle when they relate their story, who have been stopped at military roadblocks and questioned, sometimes with weird little macho threats thrown in, about whether or not they are carrying vast amounts of drugs in their pockets.

I have not met with any military checkpoints in this part of Mexico, though I have had to deal with three or four of them in the state of Guerrero. Despite the fact that they are very strange in a lot of ways, the checkpoints are to be taken seriously. Don't break into any monologues about them not being able to do this because, by damn, you're an American citizen!

A good thing to do in Batopilas, and this is a good thing to do in small towns all over Mexico, is to check in with the mayor upon arrival. Just stop in to let him know who you are and what you're up to. Tell him you have an interest in photographing rivers, or whatever. Ask if there are any areas he would recommend visiting and any that you should stay away from. You will be told exactly what areas are off-limits.

Sun. Be extremely careful of sunburn, even in the dead of winter, maybe even especially in the dead of winter because many visitors from northern climes will be arriving on the scene seriously white. I am a person who tans easily and burns only under extreme circumstances. And I have been scorched in Copper Canyon Country. Protect yourself with hat, sunscreen and long-sleeved clothing.

Enough of the preliminaries, let's hit the trail.

◄►

Tarahumara artisan store in Creel.   *Photo by Gay Gangel-Fayhee.*

Creel, Your Gateway To Copper Canyon Country

Creel is a dusty — or muddy, depending on the precipitation situation — slag heap of a boondock burg that just happens to be sitting smack dab in the middle of one of the most geo-physically and culturally wonderful places in the known universe: the Sierra Tarahumara, 10,000-foot, plus or minus, rounded mountains that are part of the Sierra Madre Occidental.

Creel is not, despite what many tourist-type magazine stories have said to the contrary, mere spitting distance from any of the barrancas. The closest canyon view is at least 12 miles away. It is, however, the most noteworthy orientation point for Copper Canyon Country, even if you start your hike from somewhere else, which you probably will.

Nor is Creel "hip" in any sense of the word. There are no funky bistros with interesting travelers from all over the planet sitting around swapping lies about exotic locales with unpronounceable names. Creel is no oasis of the road. It *is* the road.

This is not to say that Creel is totally without its redeeming values. Quite the contrary. I have come to love this place — but, like heavy ales and Mozart's "Requiem," it was an acquired taste.

Creel is the kind of rough-and-tumble frontier town that those of us who shop for clothes solely at places like Banana Republic and L. L. Bean envision — maybe even fantasize — ourselves feeling perfectly at home in. (By the way, it is tempting to pronounce Creel as a two-syllable word: CREE-uhl. In Spanish, it is distinctly a mono-syllable, pronounced CRIL, with the "i" having an almost piercingly long "e" sound.)

Because Creel is on the world-famous Chihuahua-Pacific Railroad, about six hours, depending on the mood of the railroad gods, from Chihuahua City and eight from Los Mochis, thousands of gringo tourists, covering the gamut from hard-core backpackers to senior citizen travel club members, end up spending time here. But a fairly low percentage of these visitors really tap into Creel's potential. They do little more than get off the train, go to their hotel rooms, take a short, guided day-trip, rummage through a couple of Tarahumara gift shops and get back on the train, sometimes very eagerly, the next morning.

In part, that's because Creel's roots lie not in catering to visitors, but, rather, in silver mining and timber harvesting. The natural-resources-based economy has made Chihuahua Mexico's most-affluent state, and, since Creel can be considered, at the very least, a vertebra in the backbone of Chihuahua's wealth, there never has been much of a need to premeditatingly cultivate a tourist trade. As a result, Creel has only recently seen its first paved road — which actually bypasses this town of about 8,000 residents.

Founded in 1907 as a railroad town, Creel was named after Enrique Creel, who was twice governor of the state of Chihuahua. Until the early 1960s, when the C-P railroad was finally completed through to the west coast, this was the end of the line and thus, the embarkation point for those residents of Copper Canyon Country bent on making a foray out into civilization, usually meaning Chihuahua City, which is not exactly Paris.

When your average visitor hops off the train in Creel, you can almost hear them mutter, "*This* is Creel?!" as the local herds of piglets, curs and snotty-nosed children immediately start sniffing around their luggage. And, in addition to what we will tactfully term a "lack of spit and polish," the attitude of the townsfolk towards visitors has traditionally fallen considerably short of the *mi casa es su casa* mind-set prevalent in much of rural Mexico. There are those who may even go so far as to say that the folks who live in and around Creel can be standoffish to the point of surliness.

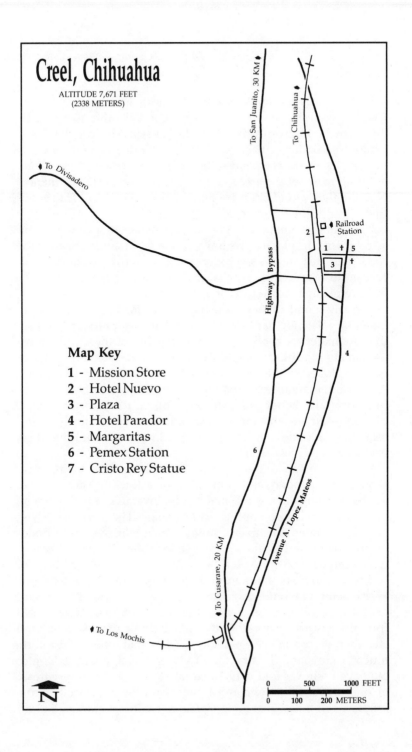

Creel, Chihuahua

ALTITUDE 7,671 FEET
(2338 METERS)

To San Juanito, 30 KM

To Chihuahua

To Divisadero

Railroad Station

Highway Bypass

Map Key

1 - Mission Store
2 - Hotel Nuevo
3 - Plaza
4 - Hotel Parador
5 - Margaritas
6 - Pemex Station
7 - Cristo Rey Statue

Avenue A. Lopez Mateos

To Cusarare, 20 KM

To Los Mochis

| 0 | 500 | 1000 FEET |
| 0 | 100 | 200 METERS |

N

With regards the Tarahumaras, none of whom actually live in Creel, though hundreds roam its streets daily, this standoffishness can be forgiven. Like most Indians in Mexico, the Taras "enjoy" secondary citizen status — to the degree that they are not exactly encouraged and sometimes even "discouraged" from entering many of the area's eating and drinking establishments. Not that they would often possess the fiscal wherewithal to enter them even if they wanted to.

What all this amounts to is that Creel has managed to remain a *real* town, despite its proximity to the Chihuahua-Pacific Railroad, and despite the ever-increasing gringo hordes. That, of course, to many of us, is what makes Creel such a compelling, even refreshing, place to visit and hang out in.

The silver and timber industries have, in the past 20 years, fallen on relatively hard times, caused at least partially because the raw materials necessary for the viability of those industries — namely sizeable trees and rich, easily accessible ore — have been exploited to the point where there's far less left to exploit. As a result, that hitherto-unmined tourist-borne currency is looking better and better to Creel townsfolk at the same time that tourists — Americans, Europeans and Australians, mostly — are searching far and wide for more ruggedly spectacular travel destinations.

A match made in heaven in the making. The town, consequently, is undergoing something of a facelift. Many of the adobe buildings along the main drag, Avenida Lopez Mateos, have been re-stuccoed in the last few years. The town plaza has been overhauled a couple of times. Much work has been done on the town's water and sewer systems. Many of the potholes, which can easily be mistaken for one of the area's major canyons — I mean, tourists stand around taking pictures of these things — are being filled in.

At the same time, it seems the locals are becoming more friendly toward visitors. And I don't think it's faked in any chamber of commerce sponsored "don't-hate-the-tourists-too-much" campaign. The first time I visited Creel, about 1983, my blue-eyed self was told in no uncertain terms by the proprietress of one of the nicest and most successful lodging facilities for hundreds of miles, that Americans are creatures more suited to four legs than two.

On that first visit, I walked into the local billiards hall, all ready to engage in some low-rent cross-cultural male bonding, took one look around the establishment, decided "wrong place, wrong time," and started to back slowly out as the patrons thereabouts, most of whom, if memory serves me correctly, had scars on their faces, sent a class-action telegraphic message that said, in no uncertain terms, "Best be heading up the road, gringo, lest ye be gutted briskly."

This irritated me. So I stormed back in, grabbed hold of the biggest, ugliest, *smelliest* guy in there and I slammed him against the wall so hard that it cracked the plaster. You can still see the damage today. Just kidding. Actually, I just squeaked like PeeWee Herman, "Oh no!" and ran away from the place at a dead sprint. Anyhow, that was years ago.

In the interim, things have mellowed considerably. The local business community is reaching out to tourists like never before. Many of the store signs in Creel now have English translations hanging next to them. A few even have German translations. And I've even shot several fairly pleasant games of pool in that same billiards hall.

While many of us may look at this facelift and demeanor metamorphosis as a sign that the Creel we know and respect is heading down the tubes towards civility and couth, there is little risk that outsiders will start confusing Creel with, say Ixtapa or San Miguel de Allende. The place is simply too fundamentally sloppy.

There's only one near-fancy hotel in town, the Parador de la Montaña, and it's more on a level with Quality Inn than with Marriott. If you want to eat at a restaurant where the ambience will more or less not offend Denny's-honed sensibilities, again, you've got but one choice. You guessed it, the Parador. If you want to go out for a night on the town, there's only one place. (You're ahead of me on this one, aren't you?) The Parador.

And many of those facelift features are not exactly threatening the preferences of those who liked Creel the way it was. The water and sewage improvements have raised the system up to the point of being unreliable only 75 percent of the time. The pot hole fill-ins amount to a Sisyphus-ian task. As soon as one "lake" is transformed into something resembling a street, another mystically opens up a few feet away. The plaza, oft repaired, remains in a constant state of near-completion. This stuff is not exactly going to have the Club Med set pouring in, though Creel could certainly use a few dozen bikini-clad females wandering around in search of some serious hedonism.

So, what all this facelift talk amounts to is little more than an assurance that the average gringo traveler — and here I'm talking more group-tour types — can stroll the back streets of Creel while experiencing only a modicum of trepidation.

The backpacker, on the other hand, will eat this place up. Facelift or no facelift, Creel still retains enough of a sleazy third-world gee-dunk backwater feeling that all but the most intrepid of us will feel like we've gotten our money's worth even before heading out into the backcountry.

And backcountry is what it's all about in Creel. While Creel is a sore sight for eyes, it sits in the heart of some sweet country. Located just west of the Continental Divide at an elevation of 7,669 feet (2,337 meters), Creel is in a high valley circled by wonderful rock formations. Pine forests surround the valley. A huge religious statue stands on a hill above town.

Even those on very limited time schedules should plan on spending at least one night in Creel. If you are heading to Batopilas, Umira Bridge, Recohauta Hot Springs, Guachochi or El Tejabán, you will have no choice but to spend a night here, unless you are driving. And if you do have your own vehicle, stop here for at least an afternoon. Remember, this is your last semi-reliable gas stop until Batopilas, which is even less semi-reliable.

If you plan on starting your hike in Divisadero, I still advise a stop in Creel. If you are coming from Chihuahua City, stay over and then catch the first train heading west the next morning. It's about 90 minutes from Creel to Divisadero. If you are coming from Los Mochis, bypass Divisadero and continue on to Creel, returning to Divisadero the next day.

Creel is the only town resembling an orientation point for Copper Canyon Country. On a practical level, Creel is the only place in Tarahumara-land where you can buy maps. The Tarahumara Mission Store, which is right next to the bank, generally has a good supply of 1:50,000 topographic maps for the whole area, except Basaseachi Falls. Sometimes they will be sold out of a specific map, in which case, go with the 1:250,000 topo, which should get you through.

Though there are minuscule stores in just about every small town where there is a road, Creel is the only place with the capacity for stocking a backcountry trip of more than a few hours. This is a point that more concerns folks coming up from southern Mexico than it does those arriving from the States, because you should definitely stock up on supplies before heading to Mexico. Even in Los Mochis and Chihuahua City, supplies will be sorely lacking compared to U.S. fare.

But, more than just candy bars, instant soup and beers, Creel affords backpackers the chance to rub elbows with others of their ilk. As I hinted in Chapter 1, in order to get the most out of Copper Canyon, this book will best be utilized in combination with your own route-finding abilities. That need not be limited to playing Daniel Boone in the middle of the woods. It can start right in beautiful downtown Creel — by chewing the fat with folks returning from the backcountry.

The best, maybe even the only place to do this is Margarita's Guest House (*Casa de Huespedes*), which is located right on the plaza, though there's no sign. It's next to the old church and doesn't look anything like a guest house from the outside. If your urban orientation skills aren't up to snuff, worry not, because within a second of disembarking from the train, you will find yourself facing a whole herd of ragamuffins imploring you to follow them to Margarita's. These are young businesspeople. They get a small cut for every guest they deliver. Thus, you can help some young urchins save for college by letting them deliver you, even though you will likely have no trouble whatsoever finding the place.

Margarita has been running her guest house for only a couple years. It's a place where rough travelers from all over the world, mostly young, mostly on fairly tight budgets, bed down in clean, comfortable accommodations ranging from a fold-out couch in a common room to private rooms with private baths. Margarita's almost, *almost* makes up for the fact that Creel lacks anything even resembling a cool pub.

Since meals, which are part of the price — meaning just about everybody eats breakfast and supper there — are served communally, guests have ample opportunity to shoot the breeze with each other. Many are backpackers. There are maps on the walls, and a community bulletin board for messages to people with exotic names who should be arriving by spring. You will very likely be able to get information not in this book, or at least some different perspectives. And, if you are of a mind to hook up with another party, this is the most-likely place to do it.

Since Margarita justifiably asks her boarders to pipe down by 10:00 p.m., you have to head out into the crazy Creel night if you're going to have any fun. This is not meant to get your hopes up too high. "Fun" in Creel, you must remember, is relative to "no fun" in Creel, or "fun" in a Burmese jail, rather than to, say "fun" Tonapah, Nevada.

Not to worry, for several reasons.

First, if you've just come in from two weeks in the deep canyons, you will not be too choosy. Second, I have, through coincidence of cosmic magnitude rather than through any predisposition to being a mobile party epicenter, had some wacky times in Creel. And, third, once you hook up with a group of kindred-soul backpackers, you will, needless to say, need to find a watering hole, 'cause, you know, lie-swapping makes a person thirsty.

Okay, you're out on the town and, since it's the only place, you head for the Parador. Don't get instantly put off by how tacky the place is. It's a pretty good little bar, though more designed for polyester and "Hello, by name is _____" tags, than it is for synchilla with yesterday's oatmeal dried all over it.

The bartender, I forget his name, but he's been there forever and I'm certain he's there still, is one of the nicest guys you will ever meet in your entire life. He speaks good English but will, like most Mexicans, go along with your pidgin Spanish up until the point where you do something like order spider web on wet dirt, at which time you will be gently corrected, before conversation instantaneously, if that is your preference, returns to Español.

The crowd in the Parador Bar will be more eclectic than at Margarita's, because the Parador is the lodging facility of choice for just about every tour group that goes through Creel. You can find yourself rapping one minute with a gaggle of hyper-Republicans from Sun City, Arizona, the next with a group of dirt bikers from outside Tulsa.

Locals also frequent the Parador Bar, so it's a good chance to learn some of the ins and outs of Tarahumara-land, most of which will be dead wrong. Mexicans in these parts, especially the older, more affluent ones you will meet in fairly pricey bars, are not good sources for backcountry information. They are quick to toss out tidbits about the canyon country terrain and the Tarahumaras that fall somewhere between innuendo and slander. But don't back out of a conversation just because someone obviously has no idea what he's talking about. Afterall, you're here to dial into every component of Tarahumara-land and the misconceptions of the locals who, although they have lived here all their lives, have never walked more than three feet into the canyons, is part of that.

And, besides, the locals are usually very quick to buy you drinks. If you are an "unescorted" female, you may want to be careful about accepting them, lest the wrong impression be given. Unfortunately, many Mexican men still subscribe to the misconception that gringas can be had for the price of a drink or two. Or, at the very least, if a gringa accepts a drink or two, then she is saying that she is in the market for a little sack action. Judging from what many women have told me, including my wife, dealing with this attitude can be inconvenient to the point of downright bothersome.

If you are male, you've got nothing to worry about. If some local offers to buy you a drink, drink it. Then, if you can afford it, buy him one. Mexico, is not like, say, the Dominican Republic, where, if you are a gringo, it is automatically assumed, by everyone except you, that you will be paying for all the drinks all the time.

Besides a few day-hike possibilities, that's about it for Creel on the practical level. While waiting for transportation, you will almost certainly take a peek inside the Tarahumara artisan stores, of which there are about five or six. This is well worth doing. But, if you plan on visiting Divisadero and you are in the market for baskets (*cestas*), don't buy anything in Creel. Selection in Creel is wider, but prices are higher and quality is lower. If you are going to Batopilas, wait until then to check out pots (*ollas*). If you are going to Panalachi, ask around for pots and blankets (*cobijas*). There are no artisan stores in Panalachi, but there are several families who make and sell blankets and pots. Also, if you are interested in buying Tara-made stuff, see a copy of *The Material Tarahumara*, listed in the bibliography.

Remember this about Creel. It's practicality as an orientation point for Copper Canyon Country transcends supply buying and networking. This town offers a good chance to lay eyes on large numbers of Tarahumaras. Check out the way they are, as best you can under the circumstances. A little eye-balling on the streets of Creel may come in handy later — on the trail.

▚▞▚▞▚▞▚▞▚▞ PARTICULARS ▚▞▚▞▚▞▚▞▚▞

Creel

Hikes. There are several possibilities right out of metro Creel. On the hill just north of town is the famous Cristo Rey statue. The view from there of the valley is very nice. It takes about 15 minutes to get up there from the plaza. Cross over the paved road on the west side of the statue-adorned hill and follow one of the many paths to the top.

There is also a small observation deck south of town, starting at the base of one of Creel's many interesting rock formations. It only takes a few minutes to get there from the plaza. Many people hike the two miles to San Ignacio Mission, which is actually on the other side of the ridge to the south of Creel. To get there, you follow Avenida Lopez Mateos — Creel's main drag — south out of town, towards the cemetery. Continue past the cemetery and wind around behind the ridge. A very easy walk. Mission is interesting. Scenery is wonderful.

The dirt road through San Ignacio continues on for about 16 kilometers (10 miles), to a point where you can overlook the Rio Conchos. From the overlook, you can bushwack down to the river. It would be possible to hook into several other hikes from this point. (Chapters 7 and 15) There are many, many trails intersecting with this dirt road — good places to begin your own personal explorations of Tarahumara-land.

Many people walk to Lake Arareco, eight kilometers (five miles) south of Creel on the road to Batopilas. I've talked to many people who have been incorrectly informed as to how far the lake is from Creel. You may want to hitch. More about Lake Arareco in Chapter 5.

Lodging. Creel is full of hotels, from exceedingly seedy to almost fancy. I have not heard about any gringo staying in any of the truly scuzzy-looking ones, but I know you can get basic accommodations for about $3 U.S. a night. More respectable alternatives are Margarita's, which starts off about $10 U.S. a night per couple, including basic breakfast and supper, for a private room with no bath, and goes to about $16 a couple for a private room with bath. Breakfast is usually fried eggs, beans, toast, tortillas and coffee. Supper often consists of a stew or soup, some sort of starch, beans and tortillas.

I've stayed twice at the Hotel Nuevo, across the tracks from the train station. Fairly nice. About $15 per couple, with a private bath, meals not included. Ask for the room with the fireplace (*chimanea*). The Nuevo has a restaurant.

The Korachi, across the tracks from the plaza, is about the same as the Nuevo, although they do offer some cheaper rooms without private baths.

The Parador is the most expensive and nicest hotel in town. Prices start at about $50 a night per couple, without meals. It has a restaurant which is, likewise, the most expensive in town.

Restaurants. Creel has more eateries than Carter's got liver pills. I like Lupita's and La Cabaña, which are both pretty cheap. Both are located right on Avenida Lopez Mateos, between the plaza and the Parador.

As far as I can tell, after the Parador, just about every restaurant in town offers about the same fare for about the same price with about the same type of ambience. Be forewarned: Some restaurants lack bathrooms and beer. Sometimes they lack bathrooms and beer only some of the time. And some restaurants don't have menus. You'll have to ask what they have. (*Que hay?*) Or you will have to ask if they have a certain dish, for example, enchiladas. (*Hay enchiladas?*)

Local dishes are very similar to what we call Mexican food in the States. Burritos, fried chicken, beef steak with salsa, scrambled eggs with chiles, quesadillas. You will not eat healthy here. Tough territory for vegetarians because beans and flour tortillas always have lard in them. Especially tough for vegans, because there's just not much on any of the menus you will be able to eat.

Mail Service. The Post Office (*correo*) is located in the building on the southwest corner of the plaza. Go in the main entrance, look for doors on the right. It takes as long as two weeks for a post card to reach the States. You are better off toting your newly bought souvenirs home with you. Postal rates are about the same as in the States.

Telephone. The long-distance phone office is located in the Hotel Nuevo complex, just up the hill from the restaurant, on the left. Collect calls are easily placed, but there is an "administrative fee" — ranging from 1,000 to 2,000 pesos, depending on the immediate requirements of the lady who works there. Collect calls to the States aren't cheap — as much as $25 for 15 minutes.

Banking/Money Changing. The Banco Serfin is located on the plaza, right next-door to the Mission Store. Do not make any plans based on cashing travelers checks (TCs) in Creel. There's no problem with converting cash — dollars only — to pesos, but I've seen people stranded for a day or two because they've had problems changing TCs. I have been one of those people. Sometimes, the bank will change TCs only at certain times on certain days. Occasionally, it will not change them at all. The Parador will sometimes change TCs, if they have extra cash on hand, which they often do not. And they give you a bad exchange rate.

The Mission Store is one of the few souvenir shops that takes TCs as a matter of policy, though you may be able to talk other artisan stores and grocery stores into accepting them. Don't make big plans for credit card use. The Parador is the only place in town that even knows what they are.

Groceries, Trail Supplies. There are at least 30 small grocery stores (*abarrotes*) in Creel. The selection in most is limited and you will likely have to visit more than one if you want to stock up for a trip. The best in town is an unobtrusive building without a sign about halfway between Margarita's and the Parador, on the left as you're heading away from Margarita's. Made-in-Mexico products are pretty inexpensive. Anything imported will be twice the cost as the same thing in the States. Plan on buying fresh fruit here. The selection is extensive and cheap. Buy beer in *abarrotes* rather than in restaurants. Carta Blanca should cost about 40-cents a can. Tecate about 50-cents. Corona about 80-cents. Spirits are cheaper in liquor stores (*tiendas de licores*) than in *abarrotes*. A good one is one building east of the Pemex station, on the same side of the road. Best buys for trail purposes are Mexican vodka, about $3.50 U.S. a bottle, and tequila, which can cost less than $1 U.S. a liter. Buy the best tequila you can afford, for the sake of your head the next morning. Remember, many places — like Batopilas and Panalachi — are dry towns. No alcohol sold at all.

Hardware. There are several hardware stores (*ferreterias*) in town. Here you will try, probably with little success, to buy white gas (*gasolina blanca*) or kerosene (*kereseno*).

Gas. The Pemex station is on the bypass road, about a mile past the turn-off to Divisadero. Prices were about 80-cents a gallon for Nova (regular) in 1988. No Extra available. Diesel is available. The station sometimes runs out of gas for a day or two and, frequently, lines are long. You will need to journey elsewhere for oil (*aceite*). The attendant will point the way. It's close. You will also have to buy octane enhancer (*aditivo*) at the oil place.

Car Repairs. There are several places in town. Mexican mechanics are very good, unless you show up driving one of those brand-new, sci-fi-looking jobbies. Give a Mexican a 1978 Ford pick-up, and he will fix it. Mexicans, unlike many American mechanics, actually fix things. They don't just replace things. Tires (*llantas*) can be purchased here, but are very expensive.

Tours. The Parador, Hotel Nuevo and Margarita's all offer generic and customized tours of the area, ranging in duration from a few hours to several days. When a certain hike is best accessed by one of these tours, I make mention of it in the appropriate chapter.

And remember, Creel's businesses are big fans of siesta time, usually about 1:30 to 3:30 in the afternoon.

Cusarare Falls.

4

Cusarare Falls And Environs

Twenty-two kilometers (13.8 miles) south of Creel on the road to Batopilas is a shot-up and faded road sign pointing the way to the mission of Cusarare (koo-SAH-rah-ray), which is one kilometer off the highway to the left (east) if you are traveling south. About half a klick further south on the main road, on the right, up in a pine tree, you will see another sign, this one to *Las Cabañas del Cobre* — the Copper Canyon Lodge, which used to be advertised as the Sierra Madre Hiking Lodge.

Take a right a few feet past the sign on a rough little dirt road that looks like it is probably heading back to someone's whiskey still rather than to a highly recommended, 31-room lodging facility. Cross a small creek that borders a Tarahumara homestead. To the left, within 100 yards of the main road, there is a small white building. This is a Tara gift shop. The large wooden building on the opposite side of the parking lot is the lodge. You can't miss it. There's a big sign on the roof.

The parking lot is, essentially, the trailhead for the 45-minute (one-way) hike to Cusarare Falls (*La Cascada del Cusarare*). Dozens of people — some lodge guests, most not — stroll to the falls daily. This is probably the most-hiked stretch of trail in all of Tarahumara-land, because the trail is not only used by lots of gringos, but also by Tarahumaras heading into or out of the outback. If you're here at the right time, you can pass a whole Tara clan — the men and boys traveling as a group several hundred yards ahead of the brightly-clad women and girls.

What many people do not know, however, is that the Copper Canyon Lodge is also the jumping off point for numerous other short hikes — one of which leads to some wonderful and seemingly abandoned Tarahumara cave dwellings. I say "seemingly" because you can never tell how long Taras might be gone from a dwelling.

The Copper Canyon Lodge is owned by Skip McWilliams and Suzanne McWillams of Troy, Michigan. They bought the place in 1986 after hearing it was going to be turned into a disco.

Many businesses might be displeased at the thought of dozens of non-customers using their parking lot to gain backcountry access. The staff of the lodge, however, operates under the assumption that their facility is a social gathering place for the entire Cusarare area. Non-guests are invited to hang out. It has one of the best late-afternoon reading porches I have ever utilized. And, despite the fact that the lodge has no electricity, there are chilled Coronas in the dining room.

You can also eat supper at the lodge, unless all the rooms are full — meaning there won't be any extra seats at the tables. A good idea is to plan an afternoon walk to the falls. Stop in the lodge before you leave and make reservations for dinner. Time it so you return by happy hour, about 6:00 p.m. Dinner is served at seven. Margaritas here are excellent.

The trail to the falls — which are almost 100-feet high — initially follows the creek downriver on the same side as the lodge. Shortly after the first bend, it crosses the stream on a small bridge. From there on, it remains on the left-hand side as you walk downriver.

After the trail goes uphill for a few hundred yards, it intersects with a primitive logging road. At this point, you should stop and make a mental note of this intersection. There is no sign and it is easy to miss your exit on the way back — especially if you return towards dusk. It's not like you'll fall into a massive vat of decomposing yogurt byproducts or anything if you cruise by the trail junction on your way back. It'll just make it easier to get to those margaritas back at the lodge if you don't.

The trail to the falls is a cakewalk. You should be able to follow it all the way without any problems. At that, I should point out

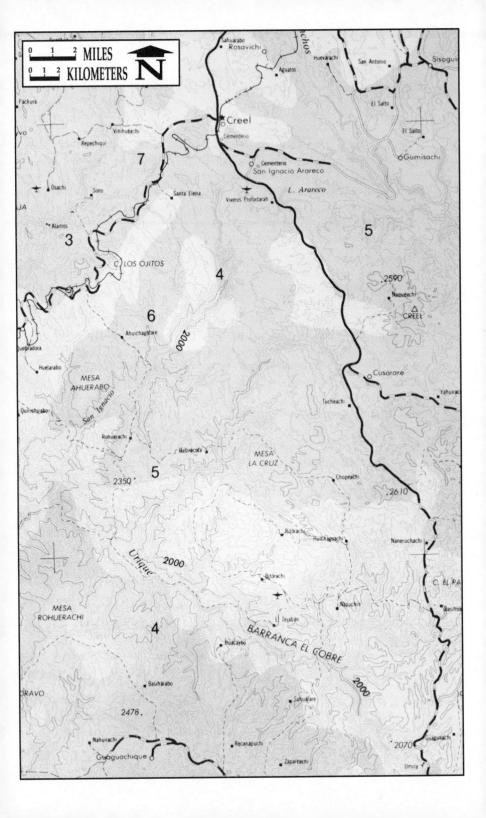

that we heard of one male human, a professional tour guide, no less, who, after being told by yours truly that, one, the trail sticks to the left-hand side of the river as you are walking downstream, and, two, it's so obvious a clam could follow it, still managed to find himself on the wrong side of the stream after losing the trail. One of the members of his tour related the story some hours later, as he was warming his web feet by the fire.

At one point, the trail forks, with the right-hand fork crossing the river. This occurs about halfway between the falls and the lodge. I've always wanted to follow that fork, but haven't done so yet. I suspect you could work your way over towards Tararecua Canyon if you followed it far enough.

Anyhow, this is a pleasant, hands-in-your-pockets and song-on-your-lips, by-the-babbling brook kinda trail. Absolutely perfect for those lacking a lot of extra time, those who are not in good shape, or those who want a mellow introduction to Copper Canyon Country.

The canyon formed by Cusarare Creek is only a couple hundred feet deep here. At almost any point, you could scramble up either side for a view. The creek flows for about 25 miles, until it runs into Copper Canyon itself, less than three miles upriver from the great bend of the Urique. By the time it joins the Urique, Cusarare Canyon is over 4,000-feet deep.

You don't want to follow the river that far down unless you are seriously hardcore. I have been to the intersection of the Cusarare and the Urique, but I got there the "easy" way — by walking down from Divisadero. I had no desire to hike up the Cusarare. The canyon bottom is simply too tight and boulder-strewn. Very dangerous. *Not* mellow. Completely unlike our walk to the falls.

Depending on the water level, you may not be aware that you are nearing the falls. No major tributaries enter the Cusarare between the lodge and the falls. The water you see, is the water you get. Unless it is rainy season or shortly after a storm, Cusarare Falls is not very voluminous. And, thus, you will hear no roar well in advance.

The flood plain is fairly wide — maybe 50 yards — but only a few ribbons of water, each only a couple of feet wide, form the falls for most of the year. Before we hiked to the falls for the

John Fayhee catching up on notes on front porch of
Las Cabañas del Cobre, near Cusarare.
Photo by Gay Gangel-Fayhee.

first time, my wife, Gay, and I met a gentleman who had just returned from the drop and couldn't believe how unimpressive it was with regards volume of water being dispatched. The falls were, we were told, hardly worth visiting — at least to one who "has an intimate familiarity with Niagara Falls."

This knowing soul made the decision to visit the falls based on photos that were taken during the late-summer flood season. Gay and I headed out ready for disappointment, because all the photos we had seen were also taken at high water. It was mid-afternoon in early November. Temperatures were somewhere in the high 70s. The sky was crystal clear. The walking was easy. It was such a relaxing stroll that we didn't give a hoot if Cusarare Falls was dry.

Halfway there, we passed a couple of teenage Tarahumara females selling sashes on the side of the trail. Seemed like it was their regular retail space — which should give you some indication of how busy this trail is. Then, before we even worked up a good sweat, there we were. Relative lack of water or not, this place is hip.

When the flow is so minimal, you can, without much danger,

walk to the very edge and peer over. At the bottom, a stand of scrub oaks was showing its fall colors. Down below, we noticed a couple of nice turquoise pools that looked very swimmable. The trail continues downstream from the top of the falls to a couple of overlooks — from whence were shot most of the high-water photos of this place.

We followed the last remnants of the trail, still sticking to the same side, down to the bottom. We rock-hopped over to those pools, stripped off in the hot sunshine, embraced lovingly, stuck our big toes in the water — COLD — said the hell with this, got dressed and ate lunch.

This should not deter you from entertaining the dip potential of this place. Gay and I are professional weenies when it comes to cold water. So, you may stick *your* big toe in while standing naked with *your* naked partner and reach a different conclusion. They are attractive enough to justify some swim-oriented rumination.

About two months after this day-hike, two solid days of rain and snow broke over Tarahumara-land. Cusarare Creek rose several feet. Gay returned to the falls to check it out. Though the water was still not nearly as high as it is during rainy season, the entire flood plain was filled to overflowing. The pools at the bottom were inaccessible. And you wouldn't have been able to stand at the top to peer over. So, with high water, you get power and splendor to stand and ogle at. With low water, you get wonderful pools that you can skinny dip and drink beer in. Your choice.

This is the extent of most folks' visit to this part of Copper Canyon Country. They walk to the falls. They walk back. A nice day-hike, for sure, but just the tip of the overly used metaphoric iceberg. Just upriver from the falls, on the same side as the trail, you pass under a blown-down tree with names carved all over it. Right there, to your left if you are heading downstream, you will notice a small side canyon. On the left side of that side canyon, as you are standing with your back to Cusarare Creek, you should be able to make out a very faint trail. It becomes more apparent a little farther up, though it is never as well-worn as the trail to the falls.

Follow this up for a couple miles and keep your eyes open.

Cusarare Falls.

*Photo by Gay
Gangel-Fayhee.*

On your left, you pass several small side canyons with impressive rock formations. Many of these sport Tarahumara cave dwellings. As well, there are a few set up on cliff faces that are not part of any side canyon.

If you cross the main side canyon and make your way up to the opposite rim, you can walk out and get a good view of Cusarare Canyon. While up there, you may stumble across a few Tara campsites. We also found a spring thereabouts.

This is an area that sports more than its fair share of Tara artifacts, but everything you see belongs to someone who probably plans on coming back one day to find it there. Please don't add anything to your pack.

Gay and I have also descended into this dry side canyon several miles up from the trail from the lodge to the falls. If you look out from the front porch of the lodge, you will see a Tara homestead on the other side of Cusarare Creek. Walk to the other side of it and make your way up the ridge. There will be a faint trail that doesn't really seem to go anywhere even if you find it — so don't worry if you don't. Follow this ridge west for a half hour or so, then descend the back side. We went down into a heavily wooded bottom, climbed up and over the next ridge, and then down into the side canyon that, if followed down, will intersect with the trail to the falls.

Unless you stumble onto the same spring we found, this is a dry hike. Including putzing around a slew of Tara cave dwellings, it took us about three hours to make our way from the lodge to the falls via this route.

The hot springs at Basirecota are about five hard hours downstream from Cusarare Falls. We have been told that there is no continuous trail. We have also been told that the going is fairly tough, but not dangerous. You will have to pick your way along, sometimes hiking on river level, sometimes going up a few hundred feet. This section is a very good introduction to following rivers in Tarahumara-land.

You can also get to Basirecota by hiking around through the mountains. Hire a Tara guide in Cusarare — ask at the lodge — and follow the first day's itinerary for Skip McWilliams' "Canyon Crossing" trip. (Chapter 8) Then, if you feel like looping, return via Cusarare Creek. This should take about eight hard hours. So, you might want to camp at Basirecota. From there, you can see a couple of caves high on a cliff face.

Another trip from Copper Canyon Lodge is the day-long hike to El Tejabán, a place I have never visited, though I did try to find it once. El Tejabán is a Tara *ranchito* perched on the rim overlooking the Urique River. I have seen it from the other side of the Urique and it looks wonderful. The photos on the main advertising posters in the lodge were taken at El Tejabán. From there, you can descend into Copper Canyon in a few hours because the canyon is not that deep there — only a few thousand feet.

We talked to a 72-year-old man — Duke from California — who had hired a local guide named Reyes. (There are two Tara guides in Cusarare named Reyes. Ask for the older one. He's more expensive — about $15 U.S. a day, plus food, but he's worth

Rock formation near trail to Cusarare Falls.
Photo by Gay Gangel-Fayhee.

it.) Duke's round trip — from the lodge, to the Urique via El Tejabán, and back — took five days. Duke told us that, despite the fact that he was supposed to feed Reyes, he didn't have to because Reyes kept dropping in on his relatives along the trail. Duke said he was constantly suspect of the sanitary nature of the food he was offered in these Tara dwellings. But, he ate it anyhow, delighted to have the rare opportunity to rub elbows with Taras in their own homes.

One other hike starting from the lodge goes to Recohuata Hot Springs. From what I have heard, and I have yet to do this, you can make it to Recohuata by hiking over the ridge directly behind the lodge. You may want to hire a Tara guide. One of the teenagers who hang around the lodge would probably guide you for a few bucks and food.

Two last notes on the Cusarare Falls area.

First, Gay and I poked our noses into seemingly abandoned Tara cave dwellings before we fully understood that such an act is considered to be bad manners at the very least and trespassing at worst. We have since modified our behavior. If a cave dwelling looks like it has been unused for some years, we will get close enough for a good look inside, but only a look. If the cave dwelling looks from a distance to be even seasonally occupied, we move on without intruding any closer. Good advice.

Second, don't drink the water in Cusarare Creek unless you purify the hell out of it. You can top your water bottles off from a well house behind the Tara gift shop near the lodge.

▚▞▚▞▚▞▚▞▚▞▚▞ PARTICULARS ▚▞▚▞▚▞▚▞▚▞▚▞

Cusarare Falls And Environs

This area is cover by the 1:250,000 San Juanito map or the 1:50,000 Creel map.

Both Margarita's and the Parador offer transportation from Creel to the Copper Canyon Lodge parking lot. The fare is cheap, but the trip is contingent on there being enough people riding along. Though this is easier with regards transportation, you will be locked into a half-day trip — plenty of time to make it to Cusarare Falls and back, but not enough time to explore the area properly. You may want ride out with a tour group and then hitch back. Or, if there is no tour on a given day, hitch both ways. It should be pretty easy, though I have seen some people stranded for a few hours trying to get back into Creel. If there's traffic, you should get a ride pretty quickly.

As always, taxis are available on the plaza in Creel, across from the Mission Store. If the cabs are out on a run, you may have to wait a while.

The Copper Canyon Lodge staff meets every first-class train arriving in Creel, as well as some of the second-class trains. If they have room, you may be able to catch a ride with them. Offer to tip the driver a couple bucks. You may even want to stay at the lodge instead of in Creel. It is somewhat pricey compared to Margarita's, but, if you've got the bucks, it's a great place to stay. Meals are part of the deal and the lodge serves the best food I've eaten in Tarahumara-land. They also have non-meal deals.

The staff will also pack a lunch for your day-hike to the falls, though again, this is somewhat pricey. Other than that, the only thing you can buy here is beer, cocktails, Mexican wine, which is quite good, and sodas. So, come prepared.

◄►

*Gay Gangel-Fayhee relaxing in old bathhouse at
Recohuata Hot Springs in Tararecua Canyon.*

5

Recohuata Hot Springs And Tararecua Canyon

This part of Copper Canyon Country holds more memories, good and bad, for me than any other part. Gay and I first visited Recohuata Hot Springs in late September 1984 with Norbert Bame and his wife, Lori. We had arrived in Creel the day before, like many people before us, with a burning desire to check this area out — but with no idea where to begin. At that time, the only map available in Creel was the Schmidt publication which, though well worth the money, is hardly the kind of map American backpackers are used to planning trips with. For one thing, it is not topographic — a handy feature in canyon country.

We hitched out of town on the road south to Batopilas. We knew from Schmidt's map that Lake Arareco was only a few miles outside of town, so we thought we would camp there for a night before cruising off in an as-yet undetermined direction. Our only desire was to at least lay eyes, if not boots, on the famed Copper Canyon.

We got a ride from an American expatriate who had lived in the area for years. This was good luck. He told us that about a kilometer past the lake, we would come across a dirt road off to the right (west) that would lead us to some hot springs. He laid a quick series of directions on us, laced with 10 or 12 "lefts" and "rights" at places "we couldn't miss" before speeding off. We jotted down what we remembered of the directions, knowing full well that it would take a direct intervention by the luck gods for us to find these hot springs.

We hiked into the woods on the north lakeshore, set up camp and proceeded to swim and sun the afternoon away. This lake is actually a small reservoir and supplies much of Creel's drinking water. It forms the headwaters of the Rio San Ignacio, the creek that flows by Recohuata Hot Springs and forms Tararecua (tah-rah-RAY-kwa) Canyon.

Arareco is one of the most beautiful small lakes I have even seen. It is surrounded by rugged rock formations and pine forests. You can spend a full day hiking around it, though if you were gung-ho, you could make it around in a few hours. This is one of the more popular day-hikes for visitors to Creel who lack the time, inclination or knowledge to venture further into the interior.

We got up early the next morning, mainly because we froze our glutes off all night. Since the four of us were on our way to Central America — this trip being but a small detour — we were carrying very light, fiber-pile tropical bags. At almost 8,000 feet (2400 meters), this area can get right brisk at night, even in the late summer.

We began walking south on the road to Batopilas, which, at that time was still dirt. Just past the concrete 10-kilometer marker (the distance south of Creel), on the right-hand side, we did indeed spy a sad excuse for a dirt road heading off in the correct direction. We waited on the side of the road for a few minutes until a logging truck drove by. I flagged it down and asked if this was the way to Recohuata. The driver told us it was and proceeded to draw us a primitive map.

It wasn't long before we were all convinced that the driver of that logging truck was now sitting in a bar in Creel with his cronies laughing his fool head off. Everyone was buying him beers and congratulating him on his expert job of sending the gringos on a wild hot springs chase.

The dirt track wound its way through dry pine forests, up and down rocky hills, past a few Tara homesteads, along a dry creek bed or two — everywhere except down into a canyon. The guy who had picked us up hitching the day before had told us it was a six-kilometer walk to the rim.

This is a common problem with folks who have lived for long

periods of time out of the U.S. They start getting their miles and kilometers confused. In 1988, Gay and I finally drove this route and measured the distance from the now-paved main road to the rim of Tararecua Canyon at 6.5 *miles*. Because Norb, Lori, Gay, and I were all mentally set for a mere four-mile jaunt, the extra two-and-a-half seemed interminable — especially because we had no idea whether we were anywhere near where we wanted to be.

Finally, towards late afternoon, we said something along the lines of "copulate this (expletive)!" We had Schmidt's map, which we had been orienting all along. The jeep track we were hiking on was parallelling Tararecua Canyon — at least on paper. A few times, we were able to peer through the thick woods well enough to see what appeared to be the opposite rim of a canyon, though, from what we could see, not a very deep one. Since our map was not a topo, we had no earthly idea if our destination was in the bottom of some 6,000-foot-deep monster or at the head of some weenie little bugger that you could jump out of with a half-hearted running start.

It didn't really matter at this point whether the canyon we had seen through the trees was the right one or not. We were out of water and it was getting late. So, at the first opportunity, we swung west. In a few minutes, we were staring down a side canyon to the one we had seen through the trees. There was a well-worn trail, so we headed down. Soon after, we could see what appeared to be a fairly good-sized stream flowing past a nice meadow.

The trail down was a maze of steep switchbacks. It took us about 45 minutes to get to the bottom of the side canyon. We crossed over the stream bed, found a non-Tara camp littered with several years worth of trash and made our way down to the main stream, which was clearly warmer than it "should" have been. We crossed and headed downstream because the canyon was more open in that direction.

Less than a quarter-mile later, we found ourselves, through no skill of our own, at Recohuata Hot Springs. The remnants of an old dwelling sat next to a crumbling old bath house. The water was perfecto. Not as hot as some of the springs in, say, the Gila National Forest of New Mexico, just comfortable enough to sit in for hours on end.

At this point, the campsite options were fairly limited, but, being pretty tired, we decided to sleep near the bath house anyway. Our plan was to hang out in this vicinity for three nights before retracing our footsteps back to Creel. Though we estimated the descent to Recohuata at only about 800 feet, the temperature had increased dramatically. While autumn was going full-swing on the rim, we were basking in summer in Tararecua, with daytime highs in the upper 90s. At night, those tropical bags were plenty sufficient.

Just downstream from the decaying bath house began a series of swimming holes on par with any I had ever seen outside the tropics, which, bionomically speaking this place is, despite the fact that latitudinally, it is not. We spent the best part of the next morning investigating said swimming holes.

After lunch, we packed up and cruised about a mile downstream. The trail goes up and over a spur that begins right behind the bath house. We passed a beautiful meadow, the best potential campsite in this area, although I have never camped there because the place is frequented by multitudes of our bovine amigos who have thoughtlessly left several generations worth of their ever popular chips on the ground — meaning this otherwise pleasant little park was swarming with flies.

Just a little further on — where a large, waterless side canyon intersects with Tararecua on the right (facing downstream), there's an industrial-strength swimming hole that is ushered in with a ten-foot cascade. On the downstream side of this particular hole, there a sunning rock to rival all sunning rocks. Driftwood abounds. Shade trees abound. Tent sites abound. We stayed.

This campsite — which I have used many times in the intervening years — is only about 30 minutes from the bathhouse. It is also less than five minutes from what may be the best swimming hole on the entire Rio San Ignacio. Just downstream, a flood plain-wide cascade drops five feet into a pool that looks like something right out of Tahiti.

So, here we were in this hip canyon lolling around in 80-degree water for hours on end. We started feeling a tad guilty. After all, we had a three-month Central America trip ahead of us wherein we planned on doing a lot of backpacking. We decided that we should at least go on a day-hike. So, we headed down toward where Tararecua Canyon joins the Urique. We "thought" — and I use that word very loosely — that it would take us no more than two hours to reach the junction.

We left camp in early afternoon. The "trail" — and I use *that* word very loosely, as well — stuck to the right side of the river. Several times, whenever the canyon boxed up, we had to climb up and around spurs. Every 100 yards or so, we would pass *another* wonderful swimming hole. The hike was amazing.

Finally, after two hours of walking, we came across a side canyon pouring a 30-foot ribbon of a waterfall into a deep pool that drained into the San Ignacio. This was supposed to be some seriously rough country and we just weren't seeing such a thing. It struck us more as a desert version of J.R.R. Tolkien's mythical Shire, where the Hobbits lived.

Though we were positive that the Urique was just up ahead, probably around the next bend, we were getting a little paranoid about leaving our gear unattended for so long. We had our passports and money — never leave them anywhere — but if our camping gear was lifted, the rest of the trip would be ruined.

So we returned upriver to camp. Our gear was undisturbed. High above us, passed a Tarahumara man, who waved and moved on. He was the only person we saw in four days in Tararecua Canyon.

After a second night camping next to the pool, we packed up and hiked out. It took us less than an hour to hit the rim, and another three hours to make it to the main road. Within 15 minutes, we got a ride in the back of a pick-up truck and, 15 minutes later, we were sucking down cold beers in front of a grocery store in Creel.

When the train came, we hopped it to Los Mochis and, two days later, we were tromping through the jungles of southern Mexico. But, we found ourselves talking quite often about following Tararecua Canyon to the Urique and then following the Urique downriver for a week or so. Sounded plausible.

A year and a half later, in mid-March 1986, Jay Scott and I decided to pay Tararecua a visit with the intention of, you guessed it, following it down to the Urique. Then we would follow the Urique down to the village of Urique. We'd take our time. Since we estimated the total distance at no more than 40 miles, we knew for a fact we could make it in six or seven days.

We camped our first night beside the same swimming hole I had camped next to 18 months before. The next morning, after returning to the bathhouse for a lollygag, we started downriver. By mid-afternoon, we were snacking next to the waterfall where Norb, Lori, Gay, and I terminated our downstream exploration.

Two hours or so downstream from there, another big side canyon joined the Tararecua. This place is incredible. Not only are there several hot spring pools that put Recohuata to *shame*, but across the river there's a warm spring pouring right out of the side of the cliff, like a shower. The views were splendid, which, as you might have guessed, is a phrase, and a reality, that will perhaps become redundant.

But, what can I say?

If you are attracted to canyon country on whatever level, these hot springs, which we named "Jay and John Hot Springs," after two great guys long overdue to have something named after them, and the surrounding area are heaven. This is the place to stay forever. The place where religious types should come to figure out all kinds of deep stuff. The place some sort of little Utopian monarchy should be formed — with Jay and me as monarchs. That kind of place.

On the hill above the springs were some Tara homestead ruins. Rock walls surrounded some of the fields. And, I'm afraid, there were some cows hanging out. I hate cows. I hate just about everything about cows — the way they look, what they do to the environment, how their carcasses taste. Their only redeeming value is hiking boots and even that is rapidly being replaced by synthetics.

But these are Tara cows and if you tried to lay the argument on a Tara that they would be much better off in many ways if they did away with their cattle, they would look at you as if you were as dumb as they suspected you were before you even opened your mouth. Not only do Taras measure their personal wealth by the number of livestock they own, but they also enjoy the hell out of a good steak.

Meat, especially dead cow, is not something Taras get to munch very often. And, when they do have the chance, they jump on it like flies on cow pies. And they are, for the time being anyhow, happy people as a result. So, when you're in Tarahumara-land, you might as well grit your teeth when it comes to cattle-related peeves.

During the hike from Recohuata to Jay and John Hot Springs, we passed one place that, in retrospect, should have tipped us off to what we were getting into with all this talk about hiking to the Urique. At one point, we were forced to make a move that, if not executed properly, would have resulted in a broken, bleeding gringo or two laying 100 feet or so down in the river. We were just humping along, not paying much attention to route finding, when all of a sudden, the path we were following became a clump of roots protruding from a cliff for a distance of 20 feet.

We made it across without incident, but Jay said later that this was the place that scared him more than any other dangerous spot on the rest of the trip. Since we weren't scouting routes very well at this point, perhaps there would have been an easier way to traverse this section. I do know that if I had been with my wife, I would have been scouting alternative routes. She would not have attempted that section and I wouldn't have wanted her to try.

Jay and I have done a lot of hiking together. Many of our hikes have been relaxed affairs, but, believe it or not, most of them have been reasonably serious, insofar as we have made a reasonable attempt at knocking off a pre-determined route in a pre-determined amount of time. To that end, we generally get up before dawn and hit the trail less than an hour later.

This we did at Jay and John Hot Springs — after a shower across the river, of course. This early-on-the-trail habit would serve us well over the course of the next week because, right around the very first bend past the hot springs, the mellow Tahitian ambience of Tararecua Canyon instantly transmogrified into the backpacking equivalent of the movie "Aliens."

From that point on, for the next five days, we did not *walk* another step. We raised and lowered our packs over slippery, house-sized boulders wedged between dozens of other slippery house-sized boulders that perched precariously above labyrinthine watercourses. We rock-hopped on slippery little pointed jobbies where one mis-step would have resulted in, at the very least, death. We often waded through chest-deep water with our packs on our heads, unable to see the rock-strewn bottom because of the sun's glare. We broke our way through bamboo thickets, tripping on the exposed roots. We tip-toed across cliff faces. We built a raft out of bamboo and sticks to float through one box canyon, nearly freezing to death in the process.

Several miles later, we were again faced with the multi-hour prospect of making yet another raft, because, once again, the canyon boxed up. The water in the box was way over our heads and the cliffs on both sides were several hundred feet high. This time, though, there was not enough wood around to pull off our Huck Finn project. We considered trying to swim with our packs, but they were simply too heavy. Because I had predicted a very easy trip, we had way too much stuff. When we left Creel, we each were carrying at least 50 pounds — not much by mountaineering standards, perhaps, but way too much for this kind of traveling. Especially when you consider it didn't rain the whole time we were there and the nighttime temperatures never dropped below 50 degrees. We carried a tent, winter sleeping bags, heavy food, extra long pants, binoculars, the whole nine yards.

We started hiking up and around the box canyon. After an hour, we hooked into a surprisingly well-worn path. For a while, it looked as though we were in for an easy time. Then the path did something I will never forgive the Tarahumara culture for — it crossed a cliff face hundreds of feet high. Some Tara had chipped footholds into this cliff, each just deep enough to wedge the edge of a boot in. It is tempting to say that whoever chipped those footholds was not carrying a 50-pound pack, but, in all likelihood, he was. I've seen Taras carrying hundreds of pounds on tumplines across very hazardous terrain. They are magical in this regard.

I went first. The only thing between the footholds and the river was one century plant rooted to the rock. So, on the way down, I would be shish-kebabed by a century plant before falling to my death on the rocks below.

Halfway across, I realized on all psychic levels — from basic adrenaline-enhanced fear all the way up to a calm intellectualism that was entertaining how it would feel to float through thin air at near terminal velocity — that I was not going to make it.

Jay said later that, when he saw my knees start shaking violently, all he could do was hope that the century plant was ready to snag a homo sapiens pop fly.

I really don't know how I made it. I don't remember the moves. I just remember Jay scampering across — I'm convinced that Jay is part Tara — and immediately suggesting that I find a cool piece of shade to rest in for a spell. I felt cold and clammy at a time you could have fried an egg on my forehead.

My life had been changed. To this day, I have a fear of heights that I did not have before. It's not to the point of a phobia, but, for the rest of this hike, it approached vertigo. Even harmless grades would jump up into my psyche and send my head spinning. This was bad because the hiking did not get any easier.

Also, this little episode altered our trip dynamics considerably. I have always been cursed with a personality that causes me to always want to be the leader, to be first. This I know about myself and, when hiking with a close friend like Jay, it is not usually a problem because he knows this about me as well and he doesn't really care who is first. But, from this point, Jay became the group leader, almost to the degree that he had to hold my hand for the rest of the trip. He scouted our routes. He would rock-hop across the river first and stand patiently while explaining to me what I should do to follow. He started carrying more than his fair share of the weight.

It was a sobering experience for me because I was well aware that it was happening. On one level, I felt somewhat embarrassed and probably would have been if I had been in the company of strangers. With Jay, I was able to be completely honest with him, and with myself. To do otherwise might have been fatal because there is no doubt my judgement was impaired. I hadn't realized until then how important my life is to me.

And we still had three full days left in Tararecua Canyon, though, of course, we did not know that. Every time we saw a side canyon up ahead, our hearts raced, hoping against hope that we were about to hit the Urique. Always, we were let down. The worst part was the growing fear that, if things got much more difficult, we would have to turn around. Or else try to escape from the canyon over one of the rims which, by this time, were over 4,000 feet above us.

During all this, we saw a fair number of Tarahumaras. Whenever the canyon opened up to more than six feet, sure enough, a Tara *ranchito* would be there, complete with herds of goats and cattle and fruit orchards.

We asked every Tara we saw if it was physically possible to follow the Rio San Ignacio, by now a fairly good-sized river, as far down as the Urique. Everyone answered in a perplexed affirmative.

Finally, at about lunchtime one day, we ran into a Tara man who told us he had left the Urique that very morning. We had been picking our way through a particularly nasty boulder jam that forced us to lower our packs with rope to a small ledge before we could lower them to the ground. That done, we collapsed from exhaustion on a small beach. We rested for about ten minutes, during which time we snacked a little. When we got up to leave, we saw the Tara man. He had been sitting less then 15 feet from us the whole time.

Much to our relief, this man told us the walk to the Urique was a cool breeze. Even factoring in an intense idiot gringo factor, we figured we would be able to make it by the next day.

We watched as the Tara man headed upriver, from where we had just come. He took a completely different route, however, and the section that had taken us almost half an hour to traverse, he knocked off in less than half a minute. We were getting deflated. But, at least we thought we were getting there. By tomorrow, we *should* make it to the Urique.

We made it the day after — almost two full days to cover a distance the Tara man had covered in half a day. During those days, we stopped talking about all the usual things male backpackers talk about when they're away from females out in the woods. Which is mainly, of course, females. As a matter of fact, we almost stopped talking altogether. Our hike became a purely mechanical operation designed entirely for survival. Though we would occasionally comment on a particularly nice agave or an exceptional swimming hole, our appreciation of mother nature in this context was limited to awe at her power rather than happiness at her creative abilities.

Our last night in Tararecua Canyon, though at the time we did not know it was our last night, was long and restless. The

*Gay Gangel-Fayhee at campsite just downriver from
Recohuata Hot Springs in Tararecua Canyon.*

canyon walls were so close we felt claustrophobic. The air was
still. At dawn, we both talked about our dreams. Both of us had
dreamt that we would not make it out of Tararecua Canyon.

My dreams were intensified by the fact that before retiring for
the night, I had noticed that one of my boots had ripped out
somewhere along the line. The sole was hanging halfway off. I
tied it back on with a spare bootlace and hoped for the best —
always a stupid hope. We decided then and there that, if we did
not reach the Urique by nightfall, we would attempt to climb
out over the rim.

I went up a small side canyon to relieve myself. Halfway
through the process, I looked over and found myself staring at
a Tara burial cave. Inside was a clothed Tara corpse. In the history
of humankind, no man has finished the biological elimination
process with more vim and vigor. Within seconds, I was back in
camp ready to get on the trail.

The day started badly. We picked a route through thick undergrowth down the right side of the river. After 30 minutes, we
were forced to return almost to where we had camped and start
over, this time following the left shore.

And then it happened. We passed out of Tararecua Canyon

and entered Copper Canyon proper — six full days after we left
Creel. I guarantee that Moses and the Hebrew hordes' reaction
to finally seeing the promised land was tame by comparison.
We whooped and hollered and danced around for 15 or 20 minutes — all the time being scrutinized by a Tara goatherd on the
hill behind us who probably thought those damned gringos have
been stealing our peyote again.

There were several Tara homesteads on the Urique. We walked
up a steep hill to the first one we saw. At this point, all we
wanted to do was get out of the canyon we had worked so hard
to get into. Though we still had plenty of food, we decided to
pass on the downriver walk to the village of Urique. This, I
learned later, would have been impossible anyhow, because the
Urique canyon boxes up so tight that it is impassible for about
20 miles.

At the time, we did not know that it is very bad manners to
simply walk up to a Tara abode. But, had we known, we wouldn't
have cared. We *needed* to find out how to get to Divisadero, social
graces be damned, just this one time.

The man of the house was not home. His wife and mother-in-
law were. Bad news. Most older Tara women don't speak any
Spanish. We tried hard, but were unable to communicate with
them. They, however, *were* able to communicate with us. They
wanted us to split, pronto. Dejected, we cruised.

Shortly thereafter, we stumbled onto Marcelio Bautista's
spread, a place I have visited several times since. Marcelio is a
good ol' boy in his 30s. His winter estate is a paradisiacal 20-by-20-
foot, one-room rock hut on a mesita just above the Urique. Behind
the abode there is a multi-thousand-foot cliff face and, in front,
there's a 30-foot deep, 100-yard-by-50-yard swimming hole Just
a few days back, I had thought the Rio San Ignacio sported the
best swimming holes in the known universe. The most miniscule
holes on the Urique put the San Ignacio's best to shame. And
this is no insult to the San Ignacio.

Marcelio lives here during the winter months with his wife,
his mother-in-law, his ten children, 75 goats, several burros, 15
head of cattle and a large flock of chickens. Because of his livestock, Marcelio is one well-to-do Tarahumara. Like all Taras who
dwell in the canyon depths, the Bautistas head for the high

country come late spring because, from then until mid-September, the heat becomes unbearable.

The fact that we had backpacked down Tararecua Canyon was one of the funniest things Marcelio had heard in months. When he related this to his family in Tarahumara-ese, they all laughed long and hard. When they finally settled down, they looked at us quizzically, like all the rumors they had heard about the fair-haired nabobs from the north were proven to be the gospel by this one data transmission.

Despite having lived his whole life close to the mouth of Tararecua Canyon, Marcelio had never hiked up there. "Too rocky," he deadpanned, implying that we were, perhaps, not exactly Rhodes Scholar material.

We couldn't have cared less what they thought. We wanted information, pure and simple. Could we hike to Divisadero from here?

Yes.

Which way?

Walk down the river a ways, take a right, and climb out of the canyon. Can't miss it.

Okay.

We unloaded our excess food on the Bautistas and gave the children a couple gifts — pen and paper, candy, a whistle.

I knew from the train trip to Los Mochis that from Divisadero, you could see the Urique. So it only figured that, from somewhere on the Urique, you could see Divisadero. All we had to do was walk until we found that place.

At least here we *could* walk. Quite an improvement. That aside, we both knew we were doomed. There was no way, the way this trip had been going, that we were going to stroll mellowly down the second-deepest canyon on the continent for a few hours, until we spied a speck of a hotel ten miles away and 5,000 feet up.

Then, to top everything off, we both had a mirage. Right there on the side of the river was a small backpacking tent. We walked over and touched it. It was a serious, professional mirage, because it was tactile as well as visual. Then, three Mexican men walked around the corner. They were as surprised to see us as we were to see them — especially because, judging from their body language, these men were far more than just drinking buddies. They were seriously smooching as they walked. We wanted to run over and kiss them on the lips just for being alive and here in the bottom of this huge canyon, but, under the circumstances, we decided that act might be misinterpreted. These poor guys just stood there and stared, their heretofore passionate embraces falling by the wayside. They must have been wondering where in the *hell* do you have to go to get some privacy.

They happily pointed the way to Divisadero. We walked back upriver and set up camp. Before dawn the next morning, we were hiking out of Copper Canyon. Ten hours later, we were staring down from the scenic overlook above Divisadero. (Chapter 6 details the route.)

We had managed to make it there before the last train. Jay's pants were torn so badly that they were indecent, so he quickly pulled them off and unloaded everything out of his pack looking for his spare pair. The exact second he had everything out, the train pulled up. Jay threw his stuff back in the pack and we commenced sprinting. This is something our bodies did not appreciate. But, at the same time, our bodies *did* want beers and tacos. So, we made it, with three minutes to spare.

By the time we plopped down into our seats, we were talking about the ridiculous nature of the entire avocation of backpacking. Copper Canyon, which we had started referring to as the "Valley of Death," had whipped us bad. We were beaten men. For several days I had been shouting oaths to any cut-rate deity dumb enough to lend an ear. Stuff like, "Just get me outta here in one piece and I *swear* I'll give up vodka and beer and tequila and skirt chasing and cigar smoking and poker and you will never ever see a pack on this back again because I'll be spending all my spare time helping homeless people and praying in church...."

Well, as we all know, backpack junkies tend to put little stock, once they're out of harm's way, in duress-induced oaths. Both of us knew we would be back. Copper Canyon is just too special a place to let a little lesson in humility jade one's view forevermore.

▐▞▞▞▞▞▞▞▞▞ PARTICULARS ▞▞▞▞▞▞▞▞▞▐

Recohuata Hot Springs And Tararecua Canyon

You will need the 1:50,000 Creel and San Jose Guacayvo (sometimes indexed as "San Luis) maps, or the 1:250,000 San Juanito map.

It is very difficult to describe how to get from the highway between Creel and Batopilas to Recohuata Hot Springs because new logging roads are cut in there all the time. I have been back along this route four times, and each time, the route looked at least slightly different.

But, here goes. Take a right just past the 10-kilometer marker, a couple of kilometers south of Lake Arareco. You will not, at this point, be on an interstate highway. Stay on the main track. At 2.8 miles (4.5 kilometers), take a left at the fork. At 3.5 miles (5.6 kilometers), you will be able to see glimpses of Tararecua Canyon through the trees on the right. At four miles, (6.4 kilometers), you pass close to a couple of cabins in a small valley. Bear right and cross over the creek bed. Follow the track up the hill. At five miles (8 kilometers), take a right at the fork. At six miles (9.6 kilometers), take a right. Continue straight to the prominent side canyon. From here, the trail down sticks to the right side of the canyon as you look into it. If you are driving here, you will definitely need a high-clearance vehicle. Four-wheel-drive is also handy.

Your best bet is to hook up with a group at Margarita's in Creel. She runs tours to the canyon rim — about 45 minutes walking from the hot springs — almost every day. Cost is only a few bucks. Then, whenever you want to come out, you can catch a ride back with that day's tour group. If for some reason you have to walk out, pay attention on your way in. And, remember, the walk out is long, hot and dry. Unless it rains. Or snows. Then it will be long, wet and cold. Either way, the hike out will not be the highlight of your trip. Hitchhiking back into Creel once you get to the main road should be easy.

I have never tried hiking to Recohuata by following the Rio San Ignacio all the way from Lake Arareco. Perhaps this can be done.

As well, in the previous chapter, I mentioned that you can get to Recohuata from the Copper Canyon Lodge. You would be well-advised to hire a guide, but if you're in the mood for some map and compass work, this should be a relatively safe route to explore.

To visit the lower reaches of Tararecua Canyon, where it enters the Urique, leave from Divisadero. This route is described in Chapter 6.

As well, the route from the Copper Canyon Lodge to Divisadero — Skip McWilliams' "Canyon Crossing" — intersects Tararecua Canyon. See details in Chapter 8.

Remember, anytime you follow rivers in Copper Canyon Country, you are asking for a tough row to hoe. This is fine, if that's what you're looking for. If it is, you need to pack very light. Bring some good rope for lowering your packs. If you have good climbing skills, you should be able to follow Tararecua Canyon all the way to the Urique. Wear good, light-weight boots with new soles. And, most importantly, keep your wits about you just like you would if you were scaling a major peak.

If you are not looking to risk life and limb 100 times a minute, don't follow the Rio San Ignacio downstream any further than Jay and John Hot Springs.

◄►

Juan Bautista and John Fayhee on the trail to
the Tarahumara ranchito of Pamachi.
Photo by Gay Gangel-Fayhee.

6

Rim To Rim, From Divisadero To Pamachi Via The Rio Urique

When I first proposed a story about the Copper Canyon region to the editors of *Backpacker* magazine, they were a little skeptical. Although enthusiastic about the fact that this area is relatively unexplored and presents the opportunity for any and all Type-A readers to risk life and limb, the editors were casually wondering, based upon my account of our Tararecua trek, whether they should be actively encouraging families of four from the 'burbs to go within 600 miles of this place.

Doing my best to get the assignment, I did the only thing any mercenary writer anywhere would do: I lied like six pigs. "Oh, yeah," says I, "Tararecua Canyon is but one of the myriad options down there."

All this time, I, myself, am experiencing a near-terminal case of sphincter puckering at the very thought of going back into the "Valley of Death." This fear was multiplied by the fact that, having stretched the truth in my communications with the editors, I was certain to experience a serious karmic retaliation the instant I so much as stuck my big toe back in Copper Canyon.

At the same time, I knew that I would have to come up with a story titled something like "50 Easy Copper Canyon Nature

Strolls For Brownie Troops From Toledo," because the *Backpacker* editors had made it very clear that the story had to make the place seem attractive and accessible to your average backpacker. Yet, there was no doubt in my mind, after I got the assignment, that my tale would be written from the intensive care ward in Chihuahua City because I had performed a screecher off the very first cliff.

I'll jump ahead of myself here and say that this attitude was a waste of good fear. It was almost as if the Tararecua Canyon trip was an initiation rite. All of my subsequent wanderings in Copper Canyon Country have been far more laid back when it comes to adrenaline output. I'm not a man who is keen on adrenaline abuse. Occasional recreational use, yes. But that's it. I swear.

Right now, Jay Scott, Norbert Bame and I have camp set up on a beach next to the Urique right across from the gaping maw of Tararecua Canyon. The hike from Divisadero down to the Urique was, though certainly strenuous, very pleasant. We experienced a very special day of hiking. For me, it was just good to be on the trail with two old friends. For Jay and Norb, it was an opportunity to make new friends, because, as much as they had heard about each other over the years, they had never met.

The only damage came in the form of three sets of very stiff thighs. And the day-hiking we have been doing along the river for the past three days has been a very cool breeze, involving just enough in the way of river crossings and easy scrambling to keep us on our toes.

Without those six days in Tararecua Canyon to twist our perspectives, this place shines in a whole different light. It's about 10:00 in the clear-sky morning and we have been hitting the bottle pretty hard, because, we have decided, today is laundry day — meaning, we don't plan on doing *any* hiking. Perhaps I should point out that we are drinking only in the interest of ethnological research, although that won't make any sense for several more pages.

We boarded the train for our Copper Canyon return engagement in Chihuahua City. We hopped off in Creel only long enough to stock up on Tecates.

The plan was to get off in Divisadero and descend into the

canyon via the same route Jay and I had climbed up from the Rio Urique exactly one year before. We would set up camp at the first comfy-looking stretch of beach we laid our eyes on. After a day of rest, we would day-hike down the Urique a few miles. Then, after another day of rest, we would move camp upriver near the mouth of Tararecua Canyon. From there, we would day-hike upriver a ways, before returning to our original camp the night before hiking out to Divisadero.

We set up camp among the junipers right next to the canyon rim above Divisadero where the scenic overlook is located — the same overlook that saw Jay's naked self frantically trying to get his fashion act together before the train pulled away, 12 months prior.

Since we hadn't slept in quite some time, we sacked out for the afternoon, dragging our carcasses out of bed only long enough to cook supper and watch the sunset. This mesa is a *very* good place to experience both dawn and dusk. And if you've done a good job of orienting your map, you can pick out the great bend of the Urique — where Tararecua Canyon meets Copper Canyon.

Once again, we froze all night. When you're in Copper Canyon Country, you often have to make a choice of carrying too much sleeping bag down into the canyons for the sake of staying warm the one or two nights you may be camping on the rim, or of freezing on the rim because you're using a light bag with an eye towards the warmer temperatures below. I recommend the latter, unless it's mid-winter, when you have no choice but to sleep up high in a warm bag.

At dawn, we broke camp, confident of quickly locating our route down to the river. After all, it had only been a year since Jay and I had been exactly here. Of course, we being us, it wasn't going to be that simple.

When Jay and I ran into the three Mexicans camping on the Urique who pointed the route to Divisadero, we forgot to ask them whether we turned right or left to find Divisadero once we made it to the rim. We zigged and zagged at every opportunity, hoping against hope to catch a view of the hotel sitting perched on the rim. So, we covered a lot more ground than we would have had we been making a beeline for Divisadero. Meaning that the three of us, this go-round, should not have been looking for the route we were so studiously looking for because it wasn't the most direct route to the river anyway. To complicate matters further, Jay and I, at the same time, were suffering from acute memory failure.

Each of us was certain beyond the shadow of a doubt that the other one was dumb as a clam. I *knew* where we needed to go. And Jay *knew*. It's just that what each of us knew was different. So, we ended up arguing the whole way down about whether this one 15-foot stretch of goat path was the very place where we tromped the year before.

The ironic part of all of this idiocy is that there is a good trail all the way from Divisadero to the Urique. We were just too bull-headed to open our eyes and look for it. A couple of times, through no fault of our own, we stumbled onto the trail, only to part ways with it before long, because "this isn't the way we came last year!"

Despite the fact that Jay, Norb and I were making Pathfinder, Deerslayer and Daniel Boone all roll over in their graves at the same time, the trip down from Divisadero was fairly straight-forward and easy. We made it down to the river in six hours, whereas Jay and I had needed 10 to ascend to Divisadero the year before. On the surface, it would seem that the time differential would be caused by nothing more than simple downhill dynamics versus uphill dynamics — going with the flow of gravity rather than fighting it — combined with a slightly improved familiarity with where it was we were heading in the first place.

But, in canyon country, the grades can be so steep and the footing so treacherous that, all other things being equal, like pack weight, there's usually not that much of a difference between the time it takes one to hike out of a canyon and the time it takes to hike down into it.

The main difference is how you feel the next day. Recovery from steep uphills is much shorter than for steep downhills. By weeks.

About an hour from the river, in the middle of the hardest part of the descent — thick undergrowth, steep grades, poor footing — we met a Tarahumara family. They had left Divisadero two hours earlier, meaning they were traveling more than twice as fast as we were. Even while understanding that they, one, obviously didn't have to spend as much time as us looking for the trail, and, two, weren't stopping every few minutes to take pictures, this was still a very sobering situation.

Despite our propensity, jointly and severally, for misadventure, the three of us look upon ourselves, jointly and severally, as seriously bad backpacking jocks. Our group resume, though not nearly world-class, at least partially backs that up. Jay has spent eight seasons fighting fires for the U.S. Forest Service. He has hiked hundreds of miles in the Gila National Forest of New Mexico — tough terrain in its own right — and in Alaska, Arizona and Montana.

Norb, who lives in Washington state, spends his free time playing around on glaciers like a crazy human. He has climbed Rainier, Baker and Hood. He and I spent several months hiking in Central America, and we've hiked together in China, the New Territories of Hong Kong, Puerto Rico and the Dominican Republic. In addition, I've hiked the entire Appalachian Trail.

I don't want all that to sound like it undoubtedly sounds. I just mention this experience thing to point out how little it all amounts to in a place like Copper Canyon when you find yourself hiking near Tarahumaras.

This Tara family, which was herding 15 goats at the time, consisted of a 15-year-old wife toting a newborn baby, her 15-year-old husband, Cruz, and his 13-year-old sister, Candelaria.

At the time, they caught up with us, we were resting. Though the descent was relatively easy, it was still over 4,200 steep feet, and we were carrying eight days worth of supplies. Jay and Norb seemed like they were merely tired. Your humble narrator, on the other hand, was one hurting cowboy. My thighs felt like they were going to explode.

This Tara family made things a little easier by pointing a trail out to us. They slowed their pace so the dumb gringos would have a fighting chance of keeping up.

This also gave the dumb gringos the opportunity to check out Tara cruising technique close-up. These people moved as fluidly on rough Copper Canyon trails as highly trained runners do on an indoor track. They wasted no energy whatsoever. And their footing seemed perfect. These people moved like they were *part* of the rugged canyon environment. We, conversely, felt like the Stumbling Lummoxes from Hell — where, only minutes before, we had been feeling right good about ourselves.

I had read quite a bit about the Tarahumaras' perambulatory prowess in the last year. The Taras' on-foot cruising abilities, probably more than any other aspect of their culture, have been well-documented by academicians, journalists and casual observers.

For instance, Bernard L. Fontana in *Tarahumara, Where Night is the Day of the Moon*, relates, "One 28-year-old Tarahumara man was found who was able to run continuously in hill country over a period of four days and three nights without sleep. 'Probably not since the days of the ancient Spartans,' observed one of the doctors making the measurements, 'has a people achieved such a high state of physical conditioning.'"

That is hardly an isolated example. Some other pieces of Tara endurance trivia:

- Two Taras gained a certain amount of notoriety in the 1968 Mexico City Olympics when they competed in the Marathon. They lost badly, both complaining about the shortness of the distance and the fact that they were required to wear shoes during the competition. No matter how hard the Mexican coaches tried, they were unable to convince their Tarahumara Marathoners that such a short race was worthy of serious attention and effort. The Taras wondered why, since they were not sprinters, they were entered in a sprint. A 26-mile sprint.

  The Taras' reputation was so firmly entrenched in the minds of the Mexican Olympic team, that they didn't even do any sort of tryouts. They simply went to Tarahumara-land and asked who the best runners were. That was their Marathon team.

- Get *this* one! Whenever the Tarahumaras feel like a little venison for din-din, they go out, find some deer sign and proceed to run the hapless beast to death — a process that can last four days. I talked with a man who witnessed part of such a deer hunt. He told me that the Tara man was actually carrying a rifle. The man asked the Tara why he didn't just save himself some time and effort by plugging the deer. The Tara responded that bullets cost money. Running is free.

- Most Indian tribes in these parts refer to themselves, in their own tongue, simply as "The People." The Taras, on the other hand, call themselves "Raramuri" — the Runners. Their national pastime is a game called *rarahipa* — sort of a kickball relay race that covers a course between 12 and 26 miles in length. An NBA-playoff-caliber *rarahipa* will last three days and two nights, nonstop. The players will each cover several hundred miles in that time.

What makes this all the more interesting is that the Tarahumaras are among the most serious drinkers in the world. You could hear the gears turning in my head when I dialed into that reality.

Quoting Fontana again, "It would be almost impossible to overstate the importance of corn beer and corn beer parties in the lives of the Tarahumaras. Anthropologist John Kennedy...estimates that each adult spends about 100 days out of each year...directly involved in the preparation, consumption and recovery from the effects of this national drink."

This makes for a captivating paradox. To many of us, the "problem" with adopting a healthy lifestyle lies not so much with trading the rapture of a bacon double cheeseburger for the staid nutritional maxims of the late Nathan Pritikin while simultaneously spending enough time on a stationary bike to merit inclusion in a doctoral dissertation proving a direct evolutionary link between caged hamsters and educated Americans. Rather, the problem comes from trying to figure out how to do all that while still managing to consume the U.S.D.A. Adult Minimum Daily Requirements of beer and cigars.

Up until I started researching the Tarahumaras, the best argumentative reconciliation I had been able to come up with in this context was something along the lines of "I'm in pretty darned good condition for someone who drinks at least a case of Stroh's a week." Then I learn about the Tarahumaras — drinkers nonpareil who can, according to Pritikin in his book, *The Pritikin Promise*, "run 500 miles in five days" and "carry 80 percent of their body weight...110 miles in 70 hours." And, suddenly, I have a vision. A vision of an athletic drunkard's cult. With teams of Bacchus schmoozers laying waste to world records in every sport. And me as their Don King.

It would be impressive enough if, one, the Tarahumaras upon whose feats all the heavy data is based lived in Kansas, and/or, two, those kinds of statistics were the equivalent of Tarahumara world records, and/or, three, there was one segment of Tara society comprised totally of the drinkers, while the other part was comprised totally of the runners.

But, none of these is the case. The Copper Canyon area is at least as tough to traverse as the Grand Canyon and the figures Pritikin cites, as well as those cited earlier, come from everyday Tarahumara life. We are not simply dealing with athletic feats being performed by the Tara *creme de la creme*. Rather, we are dealing with all Tarahumaras — including old folks and children. And all of them drink heavily.

All of this impressed Pritikin enough that, essentially, he based his hyper-low-fat diet on Tarahumara fare — which, not surprisingly, consists mainly of vast amounts of complex carbohydrates. There are seven separate references to the Tarahumaras in *The Pritikin Promise* — the first of which occurs in the book's fourth paragraph.

So, it was with great joy that I ran into Fontana's references to the Tara's drinking prowess. In *Tarahumara, Where Night is the Day of the Moon*, Fontana, who is a University of Arizona ethnologist, dedicated as much verbiage to the Taras' drinking abilities as Pritikin did to their endurance capabilities.

Fontana points out that the Taras have raised the entire concept of getting frequently ripped to the gills to a quasi-religious art form — to the degree that ethnologists have concluded that these corn beer binges are crucially important to the overall health and well-being of their culture in every regard from grape-vining to baby making. (You can just imagine slews of Taras getting a good chuckle out of that one: "Sorry I'm nine weeks late for dinner, honey, but me and the boys had to get together for some academically sanctioned and culturally critical debauchery.")

Meeting this Tara family, the Bautistas — Cruz being Marcelio's first cousin — on the trail was mighty good luck in more ways than one. First was the fact that we got to watch them cruise close-up for an hour. Most times, if you meet Taras on the trail,

View of Urique Canyon near Divisadero.

they will blow by you so fast that you will not have much chance to study their walking technique.

Second, on my first two trips into Copper Canyon, I hadn't had the chance to engage in the kind of cross-cultural interaction that makes for colorful retrospective Third World-born yarn spinning. I had seen lots of Taras, but hadn't known quite how to go about becoming buddy-buddy with any of them. The Bautistas, perhaps because of their young age, were very amiable and invited us to camp near them almost immediately. They were, like us, planning on just hanging out next to the river for a few days.

And, third, because of that friendliness, we knew we'd be able to do some serious drinking with some genuine Tarahumaras. We had ample ammunition, in the form of several liters of 151 rum. Which gets us back to the scientific research part of why the three of us are sitting here well before noon with blurry vision.

By the time we met Cruz and his family, the three of us, after discussing the Taras' ability to drink heavily and simultaneously perform unbelievable athletic feats, had decided that there must be some kind of "secret" that the Taras had managed to keep from the gaggles of academicians who have studied them over the years. We had decided to dedicate our lives to finding out what this secret is. We would become rich. We would become the Sexy Sadies of the Wilderness Jock World.

The plan was to learn the secret and smuggle some of whatever it turned out to be back to the States with the idea of opening a franchise-ready bar/fitness emporium. If the Bautistas were up for it, we would lay a nice cut on them.

With Cruz in the lead and the rest of the clan pulling up the rear, we continued down to the Urique. We had been catching good views of the river for the last few hours. It seemed tantalizingly close. The temptation is always to sprint the rest of the way once you lay eyes on the river. This is a bad plan. Canyon descents should always be done fairly slowly, especially if you have been sitting on your tail for the last nine months. Because, remember, unlike mountain climbing, you will be carrying the most weight while heading downhill. This is very hard on the feet, knees and thighs.

I speak from experience. The very last 15 yards of trail follows a small cliff face. Cruz, Jay and Norb had already descended while I stood above them knowing full well and good that my next act would rank as one of the most humiliating backpacking experiences ever recorded in the history of mankind.

By this point, I no longer trusted my legs' ability to resist gravity. I was forced to lower my pack by rope over about a three foot drop-off. It was a choice of that or fall flat on my face. Cruz was bewildered. Norb and Jay proved once again that they are sensitive, caring sorta guys, by questioning my masculinity in two languages.

Cruz and family trooped off to a campsite about fifty yards downriver. We dropped our packs right where we stood, on a perfect stretch of beach that was catching the afternoon sun very admirably. Though we had managed to get fried to a crisp during the last several hours on the trail, we still planned to spend the rest of the daylight hours getting scorched further. After all, one is supposed to return from south-of-the-border places sun-burnt and bug-bit.

The Urique is my favorite river. It would be my favorite river if it were located on the bleak eastern plains of Colorado. That it is located at the bottom of one of the continent's deepest canyons makes it all the more appealing.

The temptation, if for no other reason than to establish a point-of-reference that is palpable to Americans, is to compare Copper Canyon with the Grand Canyon. While such a comparison may be useful in some ways, it hardly does either of the canyon systems justice, because, once you've noted that they are both huge and arid, the similarities end.

Copper Canyon, in my opinion, is not as breathtakingly spectacular as the Grand Canyon, mostly because it lacks the intense color contrasts of the Grand's geological striations. Just a few miles downriver from our camp, though, it is almost 1,000 feet deeper. And, unlike the Grand, over yon ridge lies another canyon almost as deep. And, beyond that, lies yet another.

At the same time, the physical scenery here is surpassed, in my experience, *only* by the Grand Canyon. There are all the multi-thousand-foot cliff faces, rock spires and deep side canyons you would ever hope for.

But, the most important difference between the Grand Canyon and Copper Canyon comes from the nature of the rivers that carved them. At the bottom of Copper Canyon, there is no swiftly flowing, muddy-brown river that serves as a gift from heaven for rafters, while playing the part of a backcountry Berlin Wall for hikers. The Urique, very much unlike the Colorado, is a fairly small, placid stream that sports, one right after another, giant aquamarine pools that might as well have neon signs alongside them flashing "Swim Here! Swim Here!" Some of these pools approach the size of small lakes bordered by white sand beaches and bamboo thickets. The Urique is your reward for humping it down from the rim. And it is your golden memory while you've humping it back up.

Ordinarily, I would have, by this point, decided that I had fulfilled my journalistic responsibilities to *Backpacker*. I told them this place was okay for average hikers. I had set out to see if I was merely a lying piece of spent trash, or a prophet. It must be the latter. But, we still needed to find some answers. How do the Taras manage to drink so much and run so far so fast over such heavy-duty terrain?

I mean, Marcelio, who has been visiting since we arrived, Cruz's friend, Patricio, and Cruz are certainly as drunk as we are. Maybe even more so. Yet, every hour or so, one of them will jump up, sprint up the side of a canyon wall, check on the goats, sprint back down and resume drinking.

The three gringos, on the other hand, are having heated arguments about whose turn it is to stand up and mix the next batch of drinks — the "standing up" part being the bone of contention.

While all this drinking was going on, the Tarahumaras smoked every cigar we gave them. They smoked cigarettes. They smoked marijuana. They shared bags of sweet, empty calories. They did *everything* you're not supposed to do. The same as us.

As time passed, we started seriously querying our Tara buddies about this secret of theirs. They were all well aware that their tribe was near-famous for both its drinking and running prowess. Cruz told us in no uncertain terms that, yes, there was a reason why his skinny-as-a-rail 13-year-old sister could run circles around all but elite-class American runners. He told us that he would be glad to share some of this substance with us this very night.

He left and came back a few hours later — with a full plastic bag. You should understand that we of the seriously bad gringo backpacker contingent were getting a little nervous by this point. First of all, what if he had brought some nightmarish hallucinogenic tuber that would put us flat on our backs for the next 75 hours?

Okay, we thought. We could handle that.

But what if it was the Food Item from Hell?

All of us who enjoy the Third World like to picture ourselves in a scene like in "Indiana Jones and the Temple of Doom," where the natives serve up a nice hot plate of whatever it is they eat that's green and gooey and contains the internal parts of at least three species of invertebrates. We like to think that our only reaction under the circumstances would be to joyfully dig in, pausing in our mouth-cramming only long enough to compliment the chef on her provocative use of the eel slime marinade.

However, we all know better. We all *know* there are certain perfectly edible items that could be placed before us that we simply would not be able to eat. We don't know what form this refusal would take — it could be a little white lie about how we are still full from lunch or it could be a power regurgitation. Whatever, one thing is clear: the item in question is not going into this mouth.

(Actually, this thing is always a joke. Native cultures eat Capt'n Crunch and Lean Cuisine, too. It's just that, whenever a khaki-clad gringo comes into the neighborhood, they take bets on what they can get us to eat and, to that end, they run gleefully through the woods harvesting anything and everything that is either slimy in texture or earthy in aroma. Then they mash it up, add some belly-button lint, and serve it. And we, being nitwits, eat it while being happy for the "experience.")

Cruz seemed attuned to our apprehension. He theatrically unwrapped this magical elixir that would, within a few weeks, have people like me doing shots of mescal before my weekly record-setting triathlon.

Meanwhile, I'm standing there thinking, "Just don't let it be eyes — anything but *eyes.*"

A waste of good trepidation, because all it was, was thick corn tortillas liberally laced with the best refritos I have ever eaten. There was a side of sweet potato and a side of squash.

Yes, you frenetic 10K junkies, Pritikin was correct. These people eat right — plain and simple — to the degree that superhuman alcohol intake doesn't faze them.

So, all you have to do is *never* eat anything bad, unless there are gringos in town to corrupt you, move to an area where getting a drink of water can require a 2,000-foot vertical descent and get a herd of goats to chase around all the time, and you, too, can perform athletic feats that dazzle and amaze pundits and pontificators hither and yon.

We pulled ourselves together enough to day-hike both up and down the Urique a few miles. We even went a few hundred yards up into Tararecua Canyon — up to the first place where we would have had to start climbing. And, that was about it.

Jay hired Marcelio to carry his pack to Divisadero, because Jay had stuffed it with guapa-tree pods that weighed in at about 70 pounds. These pods, which explode like a sea of white fuzz when they're ripe, are used by the Taras to weave necklaces and bracelets. Jay is a creative-type, so he wanted to check out the weaving possibilities himself.

Halfway out of the canyon, we heard some faint drum-beating way off in the distance. When we asked what the drums were all about, Marcelio told us that a bunch of the boys over yonder were having themselves a *tesguinada* — one of the Tara's infamous corn beer parties. *Tesguinadas* are the type of native gathering that, if you find yourself getting invited to one, you've got yourself a nice little addition to the ol' backcountry resume.

The drumming, according to Marcelio, was a cross between party jams — boom boxes not having made in-roads in these parts yet — and a sort of audio smoke signal. Judging from the wry grin on Marcelio's face, the drummer was letting everyone know that Larry just passed out and fell in the fire.

Being the types who are always game for a little cross-cultural beer swilling, we asked Marcelio if the *tesguinada* was close-at-hand and, if so, would it be considered gauche if he brought a couple gringos by to enjoy the festivities.

This was more than just a casual inquiry, insofar as it was about 105 degrees in the shade with zero-percent humidity — typical early spring weather in these parts. We were parched and, well, a couple of brewskis would have gone down right easy.

Marcelio responded that, yes, now that we mentioned it, the *tesguinada* was a mere four-hour jaunt "over there." His attitude was "right on, Jack, we'll cruise over for a few cold ones before heading on to Divisadero."

The conversation terminated with three-red-faced "Gee, heh, heh, heh, we really don't understand" kinds of shrugs when we found out where "over there" was. This, more than anything else, brought the Taras' endurance capabilities into clear focus. Despite all we had heard and read, all we had seen, it was still incomprehensible to us that Marcelio was seriously, yes, *seriously*, suggesting that we sashay on over to that *tesguinada*.

He was talking about toting our packs for four hours up and down at least 10,000 extremely vertical feet in a direction 90 degrees from where we wanted to go. For a beer.

Our jaws-agape negatory response wouldn't have been quite so humiliating if we had not been talking some serious *mierda* to Marcelio and the others down in the canyon for the last week. In the mature tone of voice that makes wives so enthusiastic about going to red-neck pool halls with their hubbies, we assured them at every opportunity as we smoked cigars and sipped rum around the fire that, despite all the academic accolades to the contrary, we would match them drink-for-drink 'til the cows come home.

Tails between our legs, we passed on the *tesguinada* trek, though attending it would have been the experience of a life-time. Instead, we continued our dry-throated, five-hour hump to Divisadero — where Marcelio proceeded to drink us under the table at the hotel bar to the tune of something like 25 Tecates to our 15. His smirk was the kind you see on a helicopter pilot's face after he has just power-dived you into retching terror.

As we crawled onto the train, Marcelio left to return to the Urique, some 4,200 feet below. In the dark. Next to cliffs and along talus slopes. After 600 gallons of beer. Whistling a tune like he was Ward Cleaver walking down to the local drug store.

As he was leaving, he mentioned that he might just stop by that *tesguinada* on the way home. No doubt, the drum beater would take great pride in letting the world know that, when it comes to partying down — count the gringos out.

*   *   *   *   *

The vista from the hotel bar in Divisadero is the best I have ever seen. You stare directly down a giant arroyo — *El Ojo de la Barranca*, the Eye of the Canyon. This arroyo goes straight to the Urique, but because of a huge cliff halfway down, it has no trail to the river.

Directly across from the mouth of the Eye of the Canyon, also in plain view from the hotel, another huge arroyo — the name of which doesn't appear on any maps — begins its upward journey to the opposite rim and the *pueblocito* of Pamachi. Many times, I had sat in the bar at Divisadero looking over at the other side, wondering what it would be like to look back towards the north rim — to be part of the best bar view in the known universe.

I had not heard of anyone backpacking rim-to-rim from Divisadero to Pamachi. So, being intense, Lewis-and-Clark sorts of folks, Gay and I, in December 1988, decided to do just that. We hired a teenage Tara guide named Juan, who is from Sitagochi, though he hangs out in Cusarare a lot. He told us that he knew the way to Pamachi very well, because one of his sisters lives there. We learned later that the little bugger was lying through his teeth. He knew the way to Pamachi, all right, but from Sitagochi, not Divisadero.

I admired his chutzpa. Reminded me of me. Besides, by the time we figured out that he was winging it, we were already to the point where it was apparent he was pulling it off.

We caught the train from Creel to Divisadero — this time armed with topo maps not previously available. Within two seconds of getting off the train, we were adopted by a stray dog, who decided the instant my nose broke the plane of the train door to cast his lot with the Great Gringo-Tarahumara Rim-to-Rim Expedition.

We named this foul-smelling cur *Perro* — dog. As far as Tarahumara dogs go, *Perro* was okay, although his enthusiasm for American backpacking food left us a little short in the long run.

After buying some snacks from the food vendors near the train stop in Divisadero, we headed up to the mesa above the scenic overlook to camp for the night. Since we had all consumed several Tecates on the train ride, the walk up the hill was "deliberate" in pace. Juan carried the full water bag and I carried two medicinal six-packs — extra weight that slowed us even more.

Perro couldn't have been happier. He not only had himself a couple of gringos laden with vittles, but, at the same time, he had himself a hiker — me — hiking slowly enough that he could easily get his mangy carcass entangled in my legs, causing slapstick disruptions to my alcohol-influenced walking. I went down three times before we topped out. Each time, I would chase this animal for a few yards, while he sprinted away grinning like a Cheshire dog.

We made it down to the Urique by 1:00 p.m. the next day — basically by the same route Jay, Norb and I had followed. The only problem was Juan's preference for the most direct line of travel. I would explain to him in no uncertain terms that we were in no real hurry, that we would much rather take an extra hour to reach our destination via mellower trails. He would nod his head, promise to mend his ways, then jump over a 10-foot cliff and beckon us to follow.

This is the first time in my life that I find myself in the position of employer. I reflect, as Juan is totally ignoring my "commands," that I once harbored the fantasy of being a publishing magnate — hiring, firing, leading and inspiring my minions like a latter-day robber baron.

We set up camp on a nice piece of beach near where Cruz and family had camped two years before. While Gay and I just hung out, Juan headed downriver looking for bamboo. Over the next four days, he carved over 50 flutes with the idea of consigning them to the artisan stores in Creel. We suspect, in retrospect, that he was also scouting our route to Pamachi — hoping like hell that there *was* a route.

Within an hour, Marcelio was in camp. Ends up he's Juan's cousin as well as Cruz's. We invite Marcelio to dinner — vegetarian chile with jalapeños and cheese. During the meal, Marcelio tells us that, yes indeed, he did stop by that *tesguinada* after Jay, Norb and I got on the train.

The next day, we hiked downriver a mile or so, until we hit a beach directly down the Eye of the Canyon from Divisadero. We had to cross the Urique three times. Only the first crossing was slightly bothersome. The next two crossings were knee-deep and smooth-bottomed.

This was a great day. After doing a little exploring, we spent the rest of the daylight hours laying back and reading in the sun. Since we had not brought any camp shoes because we were already overloaded with photography gear, we had crossed the river wearing our hiking boots. So, we were — and this is our excuse for our slothfulness — "giving our boots the opportunity to dry" before tomorrow's ascent.

The whole time we were lounging, Juan was carving his flutes. This boy is clearly an eager beaver in the financial sense. He had only recently learned about the monetary possibilities that guiding presented. Since, in the eyes of the average Tara, one, gringos walk weenie distances in slow motion and, two, we eat good, guiding is considered easy money in Tarahumara-land. Much of Juan's conversation during this trip centered on what a young man would have to do to market himself to the gringo backpacking hordes. Short of taking out an ad in *Outside*, I told him I didn't know.

As well, he told us he would soon be heading down to the tomato fields near Los Mochis, where he would spend the next three months as a migrant worker — for about $4 U.S. a day. Plus, he thought he could make as much as $20 from those 50 flutes! I mean, we're talking stocks and bonds and yachts here.

Seriously, Juan was in the market for a wife. And he wanted to make certain he had enough in the way of fiscal resources to set up house and hearth before he popped the question to an as-yet-undetermined Tara female. Traditionally, newlywed Tara couples take up residence in the bride's parents' house — where the bridegroom serves, essentially, as a gofer for his father-in-law. Juan had already articulated his disdain for that system. He was, he told me, looking to break with Tara tradition in this regard — even if it meant leaving Tarahumara-land for the slums of Chihuahua City.

From what I have seen in my Copper Canyon Country travels, Juan is far from alone in this. What effect this attitude among the young will ultimately have on Tara-land is hard to say.

One thing is for certain. Under the old system, which is certainly still practiced by the vast majority of Taras, family survival needs were met because everyone pitched in with the food growing, the hunting/gathering and the goat herding. Now, young Taras are, instead of working the bean fields in the canyon depths, going to places like Los Mochis to earn *money* — which they spend less on family needs than they do on new clothing and portable tape players.

Same old same old, the world over.

Early the next morning, we followed the unnamed arroyo opposite the Eye of the Canyon up towards Pamachi. After a few hundred yards, the trail started switch-backing up the righthand side, through thick brush. The next hour or so is uncomfortable because of the briars and brambles. It was here that we started questioning Juan's knowledge of this neck of the woods. He had told us that the route between Divisadero and Pamachi was well-travelled by Tarahumaras. It did not seem to us that this section of trail was well-traveled by anything, save, maybe, your occasional rattler.

An hour later, we crossed over the arroyo at a small waterfall — a good place to fill water bottles. Suddenly, we were on a trail that was fairly major. And it stayed that way for the rest of the hike. Juan looked relieved.

Our relationship with Juan began to deteriorate along in here somewhere. In his defense, Juan had only guided one trip before, and, even then he was more a toter than a guide. So, he may have simply not understood the nature of our arrangement.

Problems started when Juan tried to re-negotiate his contract halfway between the Urique and Pamachi. This we thought unscrupulous, though we agreed he was not being paid top-dollar — 5,000 pesos a day, which is about half what experienced guides will charge in these parts. But he wasn't worth top-dollar. He was a third-round draft choice rookie and we were poor people. So, we refused to up his pay, though we did tell him that if we were especially pleased with his performance, we might consider laying a tip on him.

Shortly thereafter, we realized that Juan had been hiking way ahead of us and hitting the group lunch and snack foods that were in his pack, to the point that for the next two days, we had no lunch stuff. As well, we had been trying to make him understand that he was expected to take part in all camp-related chores. He was dogging it on washing his eating utensils. He figured that, since we had a female along, why should his 16-year-old male self be expected to wash dishes? That went over *real* big with my 34-year-old wife. Then he started dogging even the traditional male things, like gathering firewood.

He was sulking and it was bringing us down on an otherwise wonderfully successful trip. So, while Gay was off photographing the sunset that night, I had to read Juan the riot act. Man, I felt weird going that. I tried to get to the bottom of what was bothering him. I tried to make certain he knew that his attitude was bumming us out. I asked if he wanted to settle things up now so he could simply leave.

He said he wanted to continue working for us and that he realized it was poor form to ask for more money in the middle of a trip. But, he never really came back around until we returned to Divisadero three days later.

Just before we reached the "rock bridge" pass at the top of the arroyo — four hours after leaving the river — we came across a muddy spring. This was good because we were really hot. *Perro* did a swan dive. We soaked bandannas, washed our faces and tried to snack. This is when we learned that all our snack foods were wallowing in Juan's digestive juices.

From the rock bridge pass, the view is astounding — one of the best I have seen. You can see straight up the Eye of the Canyon to Divisadero. From there, you are — finally — part of that great bar view.

On the other side of the rock bridge pass, you can see down another arroyo to the Urique and up the other side to the creepy looking mesa of Sitagochi. In between, is the great bend of the Urique. On the north side, we were looking at Copper Canyon, on the west, at Urique Canyon.

We walked around towards the head of a second arroyo descending into Copper Canyon. About halfway to the opposite side, we passed a lush spring. The vegetation was dense, cool and shady. We filled up our three-gallon water sack and continued 30 minutes more. We camped at the saddle opposite the rock bridge pass. From there, we could look down on Pamachi.

From this point, we could have gone down to the Urique and then up to Sitagochi, where we could tie into the trail to Cusarare. (Chapter 8) Or we could have hiked south to Guagauachique, where we could thumb out to the road connecting Creel and Batopilas.

We did none of those things. Next time. We retraced our footsteps back to the Urique the next day and, the day after that, we hiked back up to Divisadero. Though there was still a little tension with Juan, we had a great hike. Gay showed that she could handle the deep canyons. Four days out of five, and the last three in a row, we had either done a major descent or ascent. And the only part she did not like was crossing the Urique with a bunch of camera gear in her pack. (You may want to think about carrying a dry bag — especially if you want to hike upriver from the point where the trail from Divisadero intersects the Urique, because there's one neck-deep crossing between there and the great bend.)

It took us five non-stop hours to descend from Pamachi to the Urique, then another half-hour to walk upriver to the beginning of the trail to Divisadero. And it took us five bust-ass hours the next day to hike out to Divisadero. We left as soon as it was even close to light enough to see. We wanted to catch the first-class train to Creel at 1:00 p.m. We knew the Las Cabañas del Cobre

Gay on the trail to Pamachi.

staff meets all first-class trains in Creel, but only some of the second-class, which pass through Divisadero at 2:00 p.m.

We made it by 12:30. No problems. *Perro* abandoned us as soon as we reached Divisadero — about two minutes after we actually started thinking about adopting him. Tough noogies for the cur.

Then we got terrible news. The train had de-railed between Los Mochis and San Rafael. No one was hurt, but delays the day before had been 18 hours. This day, the delays would be a mere 15-and-a-half. We caught the train in a driving rainstorm at 4:30 a.m. and arrived in Cusarare as the sun was coming up in a driving snowstorm.

Winter was coming to Tarahumara-land, but love was in the air. During the long wait for the train, Juan had exchanged chit-chat with a gorgeous 16-year-old Tara female. She giggled a little and he giggled a little. And then she left. On the train, Juan informed us that he now had a new girlfriend. He wanted to know if I had any advice about what he should do with his *old* girlfriend.

▟▚▟▚▟▚▟▚▟▚ PARTICULARS ▟▚▟▚▟▚▟▚▟▚▟

Divisadero To Pamachi, Via The Urique

The 1:250,000 San Juanito map covers this whole trip, but the more detailed 1:50,000 San Jose Guacayvo and San Rafael maps are better.

Catch the train to Divisadero. If you come at a time of year when the days are a little longer, and if you are gung-ho, and if the train arrives early enough, you could make it to the Urique before dark. I've never done this.

I recommend staying the first night on the mesa behind the scenic overlook, which is above the hotel·to the east. Fill your water bag from the tap on the train. You may want to purify this water. Since there are eight or ten food vendors in Divisadero, you'll want to stock up on gorditos, quesadillas and tacos before kissing civilization good-bye for a few days. It's about 20 or 30 minutes to a good camping spot next to the rim. Just continue uphill past the overlook until you reach the rim.

You will be out on a point. From there, look to your left, as you're facing the canyon. You will see another point jutting even further out, about a mile or two away. You want to make your way to that point, passing a school shaped like a Quonset hut. Stick to the rim until you get to that point. From there, you can see another, lower point to the southeast. Make your way down to it and then along the ridge that divides the Eye of the Canyon and another giant arroyo to the east, named Arroyo Rurahuachi. Stay on this ridge for quite a while — sometimes on one side, sometimes on the other, sometimes right on the spine. Eventually, you will switchback into Arroyo Rurahuachi, on your left as you are hiking down. About an hour from the river, cross this arroyo and stick to its left side all the way to the Urique.

All this won't be too hard once you locate the main trail, which is a good, burro-train-quality trail. Do not descend the arroyo that drops straight down from the hotel in Divisadero (the Eye of the Canyon), as there is a huge cliff about halfway down. Impassable.

The entire walk down is dry, unless you stumble onto a small spring, of which there are several. But don't count on being able to fill your bottles until you reach the river. There are many campsites on the Urique, and driftwood is plentiful.

A few miles upriver, you will come to the great bend of the Urique. The tight canyon entering on the left as you walk upriver is Tararecua Canyon. Just for grins, hike half a mile or so up there. It's powerful. The Taras call it the Canyon of Bad Dreams.

I have continued upriver on the Urique from the great bend for several miles and turned around only because of time, rather than impassibility. I have also walked downriver a couple of miles, again, turning back only because of time. Either direction, you'll have to cross the river several times. Bring a good pair of back-up shoes for the crossings. The rocks in the river can be slippery. And the glare of the sun off the water can make it hard to see the bottom. But, I've never had a mishap, nor been with anyone who has.

If you want to go rim-to-rim, walk downriver until you get to the mouth of the Eye of the Canyon — the one with the view all the way up to Divisadero. You want to go up the arroyo directly opposite it. Start by following the bottom of the arroyo. Within 100 feet, look for a faint trail to your right. It is badly overgrown. Switchback on this trail until you come to the base of a cliff. Parallel this cliff, walking up the arroyo. Soon, you will head down towards a little waterfall, where you cross the arroyo. Stay on the left side all the way to the rock bridge at the top of the canyon. You will pass close to several Tara dwellings. From the waterfall on, the trail is excellent.

Take a right at the rock bridge. (There's undoubtedly a geological name for this type of rock bridge — not an arch, but a little saddle eroded down to exposed rock. You can see this bridge from Divisadero.) Follow the obvious trail around the head of the valley beyond the bridge. The plan is to get to the base of the little hill on the opposite side of the valley. About halfway there, you will pass a spring. Fill up here. Go around to the little saddle at the base of the hill. The hill is actually a point jutting north towards Copper Canyon. The views are stupendous.

From the saddle, you can see the few houses to the south that form Pamachi. There's a trail right down to them. The Pamachi Mission School is about an hour further, up on a mesa that overlooks Urique Canyon.

From Pamachi, you can make your way south to Gaugauchi-que, which is connected by road to Creel and Batopilas. Or you can hike back down into Copper Canyon via the first small valley to your left after you cross the rock bridge. You can see a trail on the other side of the valley heading down to the river. From what my guide told me, that trail crosses the river and heads right back up the other side to Sitagochi. From there, you could hike to Divisadero via Tararecua Canyon, though that route is hard to find. Or you could hike to Cusarare. (Chapter 8)

There is also a trail down to the Urique from metro Divisadero near the airstrip, which is on the mesa immediately south of Divisadero. I have never followed this trail, but have talked to several people who have — without complaints.

If you return to Divisadero, leave the river early enough that you can catch the last train at 2:00 p.m. to Creel, 4:00 p.m. to Los Mochis. If you miss the train, just fill your water bag at the hotel and head back up to the mesa behind the scenic overlook. Rooms in the hotel run about $60 U.S. a night per couple, including meals. There is also a small bar at the hotel which is closed most of the afternoon. Divisadero also sports a very small store, just down the tracks from the food vendor stalls. A cafeteria is located right next to the rim. There seems to be no pattern to when it is open and when it is not.

You can figure to make it into or out of Copper or Urique Canyons in five to eight hours. On both sides, shade is minimal, direct sunshine is maximal. Bring at least two water bottles, wear a hat and use sunscreen.

Keep your eyes peeled for rattlers as you get down into the canyon.

You can drive from Creel to Divisadero in about two hours over a fairly decent dirt road. At one point, you may have to build a rock ramp over the railroad tracks if you have a low-clearance vehicle. Be very careful about railroad crossings on this stretch. Several of them are blind and lots of trains run this line. The signs at the blind crossings tell you to stop, cut your engine and listen for a train. Please do just that.

◄►

Cusarare Mission with rock wall in foreground.
Taras build rock walls without mortar.

Cusarare Mission Area

Cusarare is one of the most conveniently located missions for visitors without cars in Tarahumara-land. It is one kilometer off the road connecting Creel with Batopilas. About 22 kilometers (14 miles) south of Creel, there's a sign on the left pointing the way east. The area surrounding the mission is perfect for day-hiking. It also offers up some overnighter possibilities that I haven't personally tapped into — yet.

The first time Gay and I pulled into Cusarare, a mission school teacher had his class of young Tarahumara children outside on the basketball court, making them practice their marching — a practical skill for any schoolchild anywhere, but especially for the offspring of Tarahumara-land, the military history of which rivals Prussia. Right.

The teacher would shout the order for everyone to "jump." And everyone would jump. March, march, left, right, left, right, JUMP, march. It was too unreal.

The Cusarare school is run by the federal government and, from what I have heard, one of the best ways for a teacher to impress his or her superiors is to show them evidence that their Tara charges are well disciplined and follow orders.

I have asked various people — in a tone that indicates that perhaps I am not being objective in my thinking — why the Taras put up with this stupidity, why they don't demand that the government spend its time and money teaching their children something a little more important than marching.

A beautiful female teacher that I picked up hitchhiking told me that they do spend the bulk of their time teaching Tara children important academic stuff. She said they will be able to teach them even more if they can get their unruly little carcasses to sit still for longer periods of time. That's where the marching comes in. Uh-*huh*.

Another person, a non-teacher, told me that the Taras really aren't that concerned about what their children are taught in school, because they have total confidence in their children's ability to separate the important from the weird, to pick up on the reading and math skills while filing away those orders to "jump." What Tara parents really care about may be the fact that their kids get a free lunch when they're in school.

A couple of Tara men were watching the proceedings, the same as us. The look on their faces as they watched 20 or so elementary-aged kids hup-two-three-ing around the basketball court told us that they thought there was no end to the crap that Western society would heap on their people for no apparent reason.

The whole educational system in Tarahumara-land is strange. All schools, and there are a surprising number of them, are run either by the government or, more often than not, by the Jesuits. The government schools are notorious for teaching the Taras that it is better not to be a Tara. Tara children are taught how backwards their people are, from a perspective that "backwardness" is a bad thing.

The Jesuits probably don't do that as much. They have managed to convince the government oversight bureaucracies that the Taras deserve to be taught in their own language and within the context of the culture. From what I have heard, the Jesuits have been so persuasive that the government has expanded this concept to other parts of the country.

In Cusarare, the school is right next to the wonderful old mission, built sometime about 1740. Cusarare Mission is one of the oldest around. There are more missions in Tarahumara-land than there are Jesuit preachers, so some of the priests play the part of circuit riders. Each mission hosts a mass once a month.

Generally, Cusarare Mission is kept locked. So, on our first trip there, we were unable to get inside, which was okay because it was a fine day for walk in the hills. We each packed a light lunch and a total of three liters of water because it was hot and sunny.

The plan was to hike east to the *ranchito* of Cochipachi via

Gomirachi, either of which can be accessed more conveniently by simply following the road. But, so what? We wanted to walk through the rolling hill country surrounding Cusarare.

We parked the truck next to the mission and headed out toward the little pass with the crosses, due east of the mission. You can't miss it, unless the locals remove the crosses, which is highly unlikely. We could have gone any number of ways, because this area is criss-crossed by very obvious walking trails. The area also sports plenty of primitive logging roads, so this would be good fat tire territory.

All things considered, this is a good area to acclimate yourself to Tara culture and high sierra topography. It is also serious cross territory, with many of the small summits in the vicinity being adorned with the Christian penance symbol.

A Tarahumara man at the mission told us it would take but 15 minutes to get to Gomirachi. We would make certain it took longer than that. We walked through the mission cemetery, stopping to snap a few photos. After reaching the little pass with the crosses, we skirted a few Tara homesteads. On the mission side of the pass, the Taras are used to seeing lots of gringo tourists, because Cusarare is on the local tour "A" list. But across the pass, even a few minutes walk from the parking lot, it was a different story. The locals here come running out of their dwellings just like they do when you pass a *ranchito* in the deep canyon country. When we reached Gomirachi — which, despite its proximity to tourist "infested" Cusarare, is one of the loveliest little hamlets I have ever seen — we hooked up with an old logging road, and headed north, towards the Rio Conchos.

It is very pleasant to day-hike with no plan and no particular place to go — just to cruise at a mellow pace with little weight on our backs wherever this particular trail happens to go. There we were, sashaying through the cool pines hand-in-hand like we were sweethearts, rather than husband-and-wife. (Wait a minute. Did that come out right?)

After about two hours, we topped out on the Continental Divide, stopped for lunch — raisins, crackers, Mennonite cheese — and dozed in the sun. We hiked back via Cochipachi, which, again, was so primitively quaint that I felt I could live there the rest of my life.

This is high sierra country, with small, cold, meandering creeks weaving their way through rock-walled pastures. Like a more-arid version of Vermont. The rock formations in the Cusarare Creek valley are icing on the visual cake.

We walked back via the dirt road connecting Cusarare with Norogachi. This road is used fairly heavily by logging trucks, but it still makes for a nice walk. All told, about four hours worth of relaxing walking through some of the gentlest and most post-card-like terrain in Tarahumara-land.

Whenever you're hiking near a mission, you need to check the place out. The missions in Tarahumara-land are cool. I got my chance several weeks later, when I learned that an acquaintance, for reasons I don't fully understand, possesses a key to the Cusarare Mission. This bit of information popped out about 11:00 p.m. to a bunch of crazed gringos who were, at the time, less than a mile away. We went.

Since there are no electric lights in the mission, all ten of us brought flashlights. Doors from the early 1700s slowly squeak open. The wooden floor creaks as we advance on the altar. There's a little roped-off museum to the left. There's a rickety-looking ladder to the choir loft. There's death to be had, for sure, for any gringos who try to make the climb this night. There are no pews. The Tara congregation, during its monthly services, has to stand the whole time. On the right, towards the front, is the pulpit, rickety and old and accessed by a dark flight of little stone stairs that pass through a musty corridor.

I head for those small stairs, pausing only long enough to gawk at the human skull on one of the little side altars. I had heard there was a skull on display in the mission, but it still surprised me as I caught a glimpse of it in my flashlight-lit peripheral vision. Nobody commented on the squeak that jumped from my throat. They probably thought it was the door creaking.

Now, why on earth would there be a dead person's head bone on an altar of a Catholic church? Got me. I mean it would be one thing if it had some practical use, like a pencel holder, but I believe this ancient bean was there purely for ceremonial reasons. Supposedly, this is the noggin of the original Cusarare preacher, though all agree that it is too small to have once been

Tarahumara homestead near Cusarare Mission.

worn by an adult male.

The Jesuits, who got their foot in the door in Tarahumara-land minutes after Columbus' first visit to the New World, got ousted from Mexico by the Catholic Church in the late 1700s. They were only permitted to return about 50 years ago. While they were absent, the Taras started doing interesting things with Catholicism. Like mating it with their animist beliefs. Though any Tara you ask will tell you that they are Catholic, some are more Catholic than others. They still use shamans and they believe very seriously in all sorts of magic, both good and bad.

I had this plan to deliver a sermon that would have everyone there gathered thinking in terms of becoming nuns and monks and making donations to my cause. But, as soon as I stepped into that pulpit, the thing started rocking back and forth. It wasn't attached to the wall. It was perched there like a big wooden wine glass that you've just bumped and you're not sure yet if it's going to go over.

I decided that it really wasn't all that important to me if everyone there went to hell in a handbasket. I abdicated the pulpit and returned to floor level, where I truly belong, just as our host, the keybearer, hurried us all out the door.

About a month later, on December 12, the feast day of the

Virgin of Guadalupe, Mexico's patron saintess, Gay and I went
to Cusarare Mission to watch the festivities. This day is a national
holiday in Mexico and people flat-out party. As we approached
Cusarare at night, the hills surrounding the mission sported
dozens of campfires, owner-occupied by the scores of Taras who
had come in from the outback for the celebration.

We entered the church during the middle of a Tara ceremonial
dance. During ceremonial times, the Taras wear bizarre, elaborate
head-dressings and masks. I have no idea what this dance, performed by about twenty couples, was all about, but the moves
were almost like the Virginia Reel — with one line of females
and one line of males facing each other from ten feet away, while
each couple took turns boogeying down in between the lines.

The jams were provided by a trio of Tara men. One of the guys
was picking a guitar, one was playing drum, and the other a
concertina. All the songs we heard consisted of the same couple
of bars being played over and over ad infinitum. Each of these
songs had a distinctly three-beat almost polka rhythm, which I
think is the most prevalent rhythm in the world.

Several times a minute, all the dancers and the musicians
would let out hoots and hollers. There was a choreographer who
spent the whole time running around with a fanged rattle of
some sort. Every once in a while he would shake it wildly next
to someone's head.

Right psychedelic scene.

One thing's for sure, these dances aren't officially pope-cer-
tified. This is from the Tara deep past, back when they believed
their own beliefs rather than someone else's. A time so long ago
that most Taras probably don't know what the dances mean.

I have heard it said that converters are always, ultimately con-
verted by their convertees. This may be true of the Jesuits. One
man told me that, when he was camping by himself on the
Conchos in the early eighties, he awoke in the middle of the
night, after being told earlier by the local Jesuits that he should
be on his way at first light. A Jesuit priest was jumping through
a huge bonfire in some kind of creepy-looking ceremony that
included a dozen traditionally dressed Taras. This man told me
that he was on the trail *well* before first light.

At the mission, we could not help but feel like we were intruding. After about three dances, each of which lasted four years, Gay and I left. But, most of the other gringos stayed, so probably we were just being a little uptight. We wanted to tap into the Tara scene like genuine insiders, but we couldn't figure out any way to go about it. There were all those fires out there with Taras sitting around drinking *tesguino* and we wanted to be sitting there with them. But, any gathering would become tense if we just walked up, said howdy, and helped ourselves to a drink.

So, while Tarahumara-land partied, we went back to camp and sacked out, a little let down with ourselves.

▲▼▲▼▲▼▲▼▲▼▲ PARTICULARS ▲▼▲▼▲▼▲▼▲▼▲▼

Cusarare Mission Area

The whole Cusarare area is smack in the middle of the 1:50,000 Creel topo.

To reach Cusarare Mission from Copper Canyon Lodge (Chapter 4), just walk upstream along Cusarare Creek for 2.5 kilometers (about 1.5 miles). Or, walk up to the main road, and back towards Creel for a few hundred yards, before following the sign the last half-mile to the mission. I recommend following the creek. The walk, though not thunderstruck intense with scenery, will be one of the highlights of your visit to Tarahumara-land.

From Creel, if you don't want to hook up with a tour that includes a short stop at Cusarare Mission, of which there are several, just plan on hitching a ride. You should be able to do this easily. A good plan is to leave Creel early and hit the mission and environs in the morning before heading downstream to Cusarare Falls. Top the day off with a beer at the Copper Canyon Lodge before thumbing back to Creel before dark.

Cusarare can also serve as the jump-off point for multi-day excursions over to the Rio Conchos. Just down the creek from Cusarare Mission is the hamlet of Yahuirachi. Hike from there due north to the Conchos. Though you will cross the Continental Divide, the hiking will be very easy. I would allow a full day to reach the Conchos.

From the Conchos, you can hike over to Panalachi — which

should take a day — from where you can hitchhike back to Creel. Or you can hike from Panalachi to Tehuirichi. (Chapter 15)

You can also hike up the Conchos until you reach a point where you can hike directly back to Creel. This will require orientation skills. Plan on hooking into the road that passes through San Ignacio. (mentioned in Chapter 3)

It is also possible to hike down the Conchos to Tehuirichi. From there, you can either cruise over to Panalachi, or return to the Cusarare side of the divide via Choguita, a Mexican town twenty miles or so east on the gravel/dirt road that takes you from the paved road to Cusarare. From there, you can hitch back to Cusarare. (There are two Choguitas in this area, the other being between Creel and San Juanito, via the paved road.)

Following the Conchos, though fatiguing because of the number of river crossings — marked *vados* on the maps — is not in the same league of difficulty as following the rivers on the western side of the divide. The Conchos valley is relatively gentle.

It is tempting to recommend hiring a guide out of Cusarare if you want to make it to the Conchos, but the Taras who live in Cusarare aren't very familiar with the eastern side of the divide. They may be able to wing it, but if you really want a guide, get to Choguita, which by the way is not on the 1:50,000 Creel map — and hire a Mexican guide.

If you really want to experience old Tara culture, plan a four-day trip, from Cusarare north to the Conchos. From there, go to Panalachi. From there, to Tehuirichi. From there to Choguita. (See Chapter 15 for more details about the Conchos.)

◄►

View of Tarahumara ranchito (center).
Tararecua Canyon is in background.

8

Skip McWilliams' Canyon Crossing Tour — Cusarare To Divisadero

This five-day trip is unlike any I have ever done in several ways, the least of which being that it is guided — by Skip McWilliams, co-owner of the Copper Canyon Lodge — and that we have a Tarahumara entourage. Seven gringos, counting Skip, and as many as 15 Taras, including two teenage sisters, Marta and Maria, who will serve as — get this — our tortilla makers. Can't say as I've ever had a pair of tortilla makers along on a hiking trip. *Can* say as I like fresh tortillas.

The fact that this is a guided trip has certain implications. Gay and I were offered a complimentary trip, if we would promise not to give the exact route away. It is important to understand the reasoning behind this. Certainly, there's some capitalism involved on Skip's part. He went out and found the route over the course of several years and he makes part of his living by leading paying customers on it. But, that's only a small part of the deal.

Because his "Canyon Crossing" route cuts very close to a few Tara homesteads that are way far away from anything and everything even remotely civilized, Skip feels a need to limit the number of excursions through those areas. He, through talking with the Taras in question, has picked up on how many gringos they can live with cruising through their neighborhood and how many are too many. Skip has limited his trips accordingly.

Though I understand and sympathize with that argument, I still considered not going along because, I figured, I needed to be able to tell folks, insofar as I mention the trip at all in this book, how to make their way along the same route. I chewed my mental cud over it for a few days and decided to go ahead and include this chapter anyway for two reasons.

First, by writing in very generalized terms where we went, you will be able to make your way from Cusarare to Divisadero. At the same time, by giving *only* very generalized directions, even if you tried to follow directly in our footsteps, the chances of you succeeding are very slim — even if you hired a Tara guide. It's not that the route is overly hard, it's just that there are simply too many ways to get between the points we traversed. This is good. You will likely discover places we did not; yet, at the same time, you will view many of the same large-scale scenes.

And, second, you may be interested in going on one of Skip's trips. Including one professionally guided trip in this book is a good idea because many of you might be considering employing the services of a guide for your Copper Canyon Country visit.

The seven gringos were: Skip, a female nurse from California, a male commercial real estate broker from Michigan, a female tour operator from California, a female karate instructor/triathlete from Florida — there's one serious human in every bunch, it seems — and Gay and I. We headed out about the crack of noon. The gringos, 10 or 12 Taras (more would join us later), including the tortilla makers, five burros, a couple of horses, a couple of dogs and five live chickens.

I had only put my pack on a quadruped once before and, while I was tending to the repairs several days later, I decided to never do so again. But, since everybody else was doing it, we would have to also. We were told there would be "no problems" with our brand-new, multi-hundred-dollar packs.

We headed out from the lodge towards Basirecota, which is actually right on Cusarare Creek, the same as the lodge. We were going the long way as the crow flies, but the short way as the crow walks with five burros.

I have always had bad preconceptions about what a guided

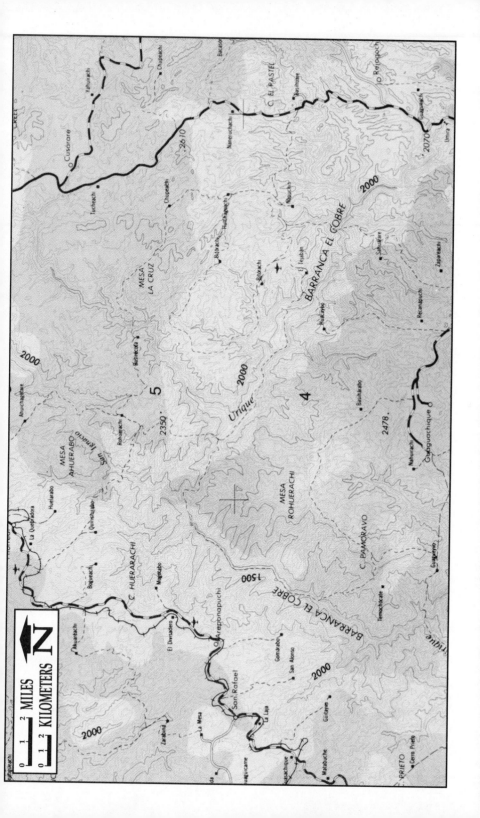

trip would be like. I had no idea whether the perfect strangers who I would be living in tight quarters with for the next five days — who seemed perfectly normal before the trip commenced — would all become crazy people after we'd been on the trail for a few minutes. Worse, I had no idea whether my otherwise extremely stable disposition would come unraveled when faced with the reality that someone else was responsible for route-finding, food preparation and maintaining general group harmony.

The walk to Basirecota takes only about three hours via the mountain route. There are a couple steep uphills, but nothing serious. This was the stretch where we all got to know each other a little bit. We were very relieved to learn that only the triathlete from Florida was in anything approaching good shape. Gay and I had only been in Mexico for a week or so, and, as usual, we hadn't exactly killed ourselves getting physically prepared for the trip. We were not enthusiastic about the possibility of finding ourselves in a group of gung-ho Outward Bound types.

Our pace hovered somewhere around two miles an hour, with minimal weight. We rested frequently, because we were in no hurry. Though I have adopted this mellow sort of hiking strategy myself on more than one occasion, I felt a little weird about it here and now. For one thing, it seemed like I was "cheating" by having a pack animal carry my pack.

My wife, on the other hand, within about two miles of the lodge, was already talking in terms of never carrying a pack again in her entire life. She thought the concept of beasts-of-burden as backpacking compadres was splendid. So did our gringo companions.

Skip, who, we learned immediately, is not a guide cut from the traditional mold, could hardly see it any other way. He is perplexed and amused by many of the backcountry attitudes that typical American backpackers possess in the extreme.

Skip has been hiking in Tarahumara-land for 25 years. Yet, he has only recently started carrying a pack, and that is only about 1,000 cubic inches — designed more for day-hiking than five-day trips. Though he has been out for as long as a month at a time, the most Skip carries is a blanket, some *pinole* — a Tarahumara staple that is nothing more than ground corn, mixed for consumption with cold water — a knife and some basic personal hygiene items. This sounds as though Skip is a bad-assed, backcountry Muir-clone. Probably sports a beard. Talks little. Rather gruff.

None of these stereotypes even comes close.

Skip McWilliams lives in a Detroit, Michigan, suburb, where he runs an educational film company. He is clean-shaven, out-of-shape, and one of the few people I have ever met in my life who likes to hear himself talk as much as I like to hear myself talk.

When we left the lodge, he was wearing some peepee-looking street shoes, with a piece of cardboard stuck in one of the heels because he had worn a blister on his last trip. He brought no extra clothing, no sleeping bag, no pad. And, he asked everyone to limit their gear to much the same degree. Before we left, everyone pulled everything out of their packs. I have never seen gear honed-down that much. By the time we pulled out, I had three people's gear stuffed into my pack — with plenty of room to spare.

The reason Skip was so insistent about cutting our gear was that, halfway through the trip, we would reach a stretch of trail that the burros would not be able to traverse. From that point on, we would be relying totally on Tara porters. The less stuff we had, the less extra porters Skip would have to hire in Sitagochi, where the burros would be sent back.

Skip, unlike my preconceptions of wilderness guides, knows relatively little about the plant and animal life in Copper Canyon Country. For that information, Skip has the "Mexican Gandalf" — Jesus Olivas. Jesus is one of the most-wonderful people I have ever met. He grew up in Copper Canyon Country. His dad was a trader who ran burro trains all over Tarahumara-land. Jesus, from the time he was nine, followed his dad on his rounds. Consequently, he probably knows the area as well as anyone. And he knows the fauna and flora intimately.

Skip is more interested in Mexican history than natural history. He is completely fluent in Spanish — as opposed to being merely conversant. He reads Spanish as well as I read English and has spent many years studying the Mexican Revolution.

As we passed through the thick pines on our way to Basirecota, we learned a lot about Pancho Villa and his *tropa* — troop — the guys who effectively amount to Mexico's Founding Fathers.

Especially interesting was Skip's rendition of "Villa on the

Cross," which is the name of a chapter in the book, *The Eagle and the Serpent* by Martin Luis Guzman, who was the clerk of the *tropa*.

For most of the early years of the Mexican Revolution, Villa had the nasty habit of taking large numbers of prisoners and executing them — even those who were willing to change sides. At some point, one of his underlings convinced Villa that he should mend his ways, for two reasons. First, people who know they are going to be killed if they are captured are likely to fight like the dickens to make certain they are not captured and, second, when his enemies offered to change sides, it was tantamount to them admitting that Villa was philosophically right.

So, Villa got on the telegraph and frantically wired someplace down the line where several hundred prisoners were scheduled to be shot that the executions should be stopped. For hours, Villa paced back and forth, figuratively "on the cross," until he got word that his message had made it through.

I don't remember whether it made it through on time.

We reached a high mesa above Cusarare Canyon. This is Chuyachi, our first view of the deep canyon country. We descended a steep side arroyo to the Cusarare River in the gathering dusk. Most of the Taras were already in camp. They were gathering wood, tending to the animals and shooting the breeze. To them, this trip was a laid-back vacation.

Camp was a small abandoned Tara bean field just above the rocky flood plain of the Cusarare. About 20 feet from the fire ring were two small hot pools, each the size of a kitchen sink. Upriver a few dozen yards are a couple larger hot spring pools. Across the river and up a hill are a couple caves. Skip speculated that they were burial caves, but this is not as formal as it sounds.

Apparently, the Taras do not revere their dead. They operate on a day-to-day basis with the belief that nothing happens by chance, that a person wills all that transpires in his or her life — including death. Therefore, the Taras look at their deceased compadres as people who made the choice, for whatever reason, to leave their loved ones behind in the material world. This, quite often, does not endear the dearly departed towards those still operating in the mortal dimension.

One story was told about a Tara man who chained his dead

Tarahumara cave art, near Sitagochi.

mother up and dragged her stiff carcass up into a cave, where she was kept for over a year, until the Tara man was convinced she was too decomposed to re-enter the world of the living. The Tara man was upset with his mom because she was supposedly an opium poppy farmer.

After a year, this man invited Skip and Jesus to join him on a journey to the cave, where he planned on retrieving the chains, with an eye towards selling them. Skip and Jesus were both, surprisingly, too busy that day to tag along.

The nurse and the triathlete went up to investigate the caves — before this story was told. It ended up that the caves were used for nothing more macabre than penning goats.

Our two tortilla makers were sitting down by the river when the gringos arrived at camp. I wandered down to see what they were up to, thinking, perhaps, I could pick up on some sort of

Tara tortilla-making tidbit. Before they noticed my approach, they had been jabbering away with enthusiasm. When I arrived, they shut up tight. I was looking down at their feet — which is where they seemed to be looking — hoping to see what they were up to. Then this little light bulb goes on over my putty-brained gringo self. Marta and Maria had been washing up in the river in a most private manner, which should have been obvious to anyone, save the world's most stupid piece of lizard dung — me. These poor girls thought that I was sneaking down to the creek with the idea of getting a prurient peak before din-din. We hadn't even shared our first meal as a group and, already, the Taras were thinking they had a pervert in their midst.

The Taras looked amused as the gringos went about setting up camp. Gay and the tour operator shared our tent. The nurse and the triathlete each brought one-human tents, and they were busy setting them up. The real estate broker and I planned on sleeping under the stars, but, even then, it still takes gringos at least 20 minutes to get organized.

Dinner consisted mainly of pig meat, cheese and tortillas — good eats for one who's used to freeze-dried beans and such on the trail.

During supper, the Taras pretty much stayed on one side of the fire, the gringos on the other. There were enthusiastic conversations on both sides, but not much in the way of cross-cultural interaction. This is not too surprising, since, besides Skip, I was the closest thing to a bi- lingual gringo on the scene. The Taras were all bi-lingual, but none of their linguals was English. So, of course, I decided to break the ice. I walked over to the other side of the fire and began asking everyone's name, with the intent of introducing everybody to everybody else. The instant I passed the line of demarcation, the Taras started looking nervous. I ask them each, one-by-one, what their name is. They answer so softly that I have to ask every one of them to repeat their whisper.

Then I begin the gringo intros with myself. John is difficult to pronounce for Spanish-speakers, so I am "Juan." Then I turn to start introducing the others. None are paying attention. By the time I turn back to the Taras, they have inched away. They face the other direction.

I consider, briefly, that I once thought I was perfect material for a diplomatic corps career. I even met with the State Department recruiter in college. Had I gone through with it, I suspect we would now be at war with whoever I was trying to be diplomatic with.

The scene around the fire soon evolved into relaxed tequila-sipping and soft-spoken story telling. There were two bottles of tequila and everyone, except the triathlete, partook whenever the bottles were passed their way. With me, we're just talking about a shift in alcoholic venue. With some of the other gringos, we're talking about a major transformation of evening beverage. There are coughs and sputters. The Taras giggle. Then the Tara tortilla makers each take small sips, droplets gleaming down their necks in the firelight. The gringos giggle. Cigars are torched. A pot of coffee is boiled. Jokes are told in three languages. The creek babbles. The burros, hobbled away in the darkness, bray.

As my buddy Bame would say, "Handle it, handle it."

Tomorrow morning, we head straight back up to the sierra. Tomorrow night, after eight hours on the trail, we will sleep within sight of Sitagochi — the pueblo primeval.

One of our members has zero experience in the backcountry. Everyone else at least has some experience, though no one is a world-class wilderness jock. Skip, who prefers customers with little or no backcountry experience, sets the groups' pace based on the person with no experience. He feels that it is best to maintain a pace that you can keep up all day, no matter how slow it is. Though this is somewhat hard on those who would feel more comfortable walking a little faster, it is a good plan for the group.

The gringos are off by 10:00 a.m., heading a couple thousand feet straight up. The Taras are in no hurry to break camp. They have no fear of being left behind. We will follow the ridge that separates Cusarare Canyon from Tararecua Canyon until we reach Sitagochi.

As we slowly ascend out of Cusarare Canyon, we can hear the Taras below laughing. Sometimes I don't like Taras very much. On the one hand, I am amused by the fact that we amuse them. I mean, we must seem like a population of materially affluent evolutionary miscues. We have no endurance. We are pudgy and soft. We can't start fires worth a damn. We bring too much stuff. So, they sit and laugh as we huff and puff.

I transfer the scene. How would it look if I sat there and laughed at a Tara who was suddenly plopped into the middle of a large mall? I could send him into a Fashion Bar with a personal deficit enlargement tool — a credit card — and instructions to buy a set of sexy undies for his sister. Then *I* could sit back and chuckle.

The worst single thing about backpacking is when you have to do a long, steep uphill first thing in the morning. We are moving stiff-legged and slow, though, man oh man, this is a lot better without backpacks. Though I am "one with" many of the aspects of life on the trail — the crappy food, the wet and cold, the frequent lack of cold beer — the one thing that I could most-easily live without is the backpack part of backpacking. But, I still feel very strange knowing that our Tara compadres think that the gringos *need* help with their gear, that we would be unable to make it without them and their burros.

Shortly after we reach the ridge top, we enter a Tara *ranchito*. Skip goes over and sits outside one of the fences. A few minutes later, a Tara man comes over and commences to shoot the breeze with him. The man runs back into his abode, then returns. They both come over to where we are sitting, and Skip introduces the man. We shake hands all the way around.

The man is vending some little pine-needle sombreros that his wife has made. Each of us buys one — for 40 cents. Taras are astounding craftspeople, especially when it comes to weaving stuff out of pine needles and yucca leaves.

When we split, Skip tells us that the man will join us tomorrow morning. He will replace one of the burros. Meaning he will become a bearer and toter.

We look for, and find, a spring. Sometimes springs in Tarahumara-land can be hard to locate, because they are covered with flat rocks to keep livestock snouts away from the water. These covered water sources blend right into the local terrain.

By noon, the Taras catch up and lunch is prepared — tuna salad, biscuits and fresh fruit. Shortly after stuffing our faces, we're back on the trail. We pass by an edifice that looks like one of those tacky scientific buildings down in Antarctica — the kind

The tortilla makers, Marta (left) and Maria.

you see pictures of on TV specials about how the last continent is going to the dogs.

This building is not, its architectural countenance notwithstanding, the fault of scientists. No, this is worse. This building belongs to the Jesuits. It is a storage facility. No windows, one door, heavily locked. There's no telling what is in the building, but a good guess would be clothing. I had often wondered how the Taras — whose traditional dress is, for women, colorful, dignified skirts and blouses, and, for men, pure white, dignified dress-looking things — came to wear, on the whole, ill-fitting, polyester, pastel-colored, mis-matched, leisure-suit remnants from K-Mart bargain racks of 15 years ago.

The answer, come to find out, is simple. The Jesuits have succeeded in convincing the Taras that their traditional dress is un-hip. So, many Taras now wear gringo duds, which, of course, they need to get from the outside world. The Jesuits, being good business types, run clothing drives in the States for the poor unfortunate, naked heathens south of the border. I've heard reports that they then sell these dweeby-looking rags to the Taras.

The storage shed was accessed by a well-maintained dirt road that was built by the Taras. According to McWilliams, the Jesuits, when they need some work done — like road building — will simply scour the area for all able-bodied males. They will, essentially, draft them for as long as it takes to complete the task at hand. The Jesuits want nice roads like this built because they prefer traveling through Tarahumara-land in vans. It ain't my territory. I've got nothing to say.

We arrived at camp just before dusk and just after passing by a Tara cave that was decorated by stone-age-looking wall art. This campsite was one of my all-time favorites. The fire was built inside a crumbling rock house formation just big enough for everyone to squeeze in. Tents were pitched in a small field with a view of Cusarare Canyon off in the distance.

Gay and I run off for the 20-minute walk to a point where we can view both Tararecua Canyon and Copper Canyon. Though the light is not good for photo-taking, suffice to say that this one view, maybe the best in all of Tarahumara-land, is worth two full days of walking.

From the top of the small ridge above camp, we can see Sitagochi, which, I guess, is technically a butte, rather than a mesa, because it is eroded from, rather than to. Either way, this looks like something out of a Conan the Barbarian film. Just this flat, treeless, wind-swept butte perched above the depths of Copper Canyon. It is from Sitagochi that our Tarahumara burro-replacement units will be procured.

The water source, a spring, I am told, is about a 10-minute walk downhill from camp. I am also told "I can't miss it" — my least-favorite words in the backcountry user's lexicon.

I head down, and, of course, I miss it. I do find a spring, seemingly 17 or 18 miles later, but it's definitely not the one everybody else managed to find. On the way back, I pass close by the tortilla makers — once again — taking a bath. If there was any doubt whatsoever in their minds about me the first time, there is none now. I can't believe it.

When I get back to camp, I take a big swig. The water tastes like dishwater, which, come to find out, is exactly what it is. Often times, when there are several springs in one area, the Taras will use one for drinking, one for washing and one for animals. I left in search of water, sweet water. I returned with three liters of Lux on the rocks.

Because this is our last night with the burros, once more, Skip asks us to pare down our gear. Anything we haven't used yet, we are asked to send back to Cusarare on the burros. By morning, eight more Taras have joined our group. With the exception of the guy we bought the little sombreros from, all the new recruits are under 17. Some have walked all night to get here in time. This is good luck. In times past, Skip has had to wait until late afternoon before getting enough Tara Sherpas.

By this time, I've got four people's stuff in my Lowe pack. I hope it holds together because two of its main support straps have been rubbing on the burro's saddle frame. They are frayed and, if they break, my pack becomes separated from its high-tech ABS-plastic frame. Never again will I put my pack on anything with more than three legs.

Even though none of us has much gear left, my pack is still heavy, because near-bouts every gringo for 50 miles has their stuff in it. It is given to a Tara who stands about 5'1". I am hardly a tall man, but when my pack settles onto this poor bugger's back, I feel like "Wilt the Stilt." The hip strap is almost down to the guy's knees. He could use the chest strap as an athletic supporter.

All the other Taras end up carrying, like, small bags of fruit. So, the poor schmuck with my pack has gotten the shaft. The seeds of dissention have been sown. Our very own labor dispute is about to begin.

Today is a big day. We have before us a multi-hour, multi-thousand-foot descent into Tararecua Canyon, at a point only a few miles upriver from the great bend of the Urique. For me, it's the first time I will enter the depths of Tararecua since Jay Scott and I spent six days down there three years before.

The descent into Tararecua Canyon was slow and hot. This was the time of year, late November, when every seed with a propensity to latch itself onto a passerby was ready for action.

By mid-day, we were all walking flora reproduction aids.

Impossible as it seems, I remember passing, three years before, by the exact stretch of river above which Skip now chooses to camp. There's a little waterfall just upriver. Jay and I stopped by it to eat lunch. Minutes before, I had had my first experience with quicksand, which is a pulse-rate-increasing sort of thing. I had jumped from the riverbank down onto some solid-looking dirt. Next thing I know, I'm thinking in terms of needing a fresh change of underwear. I was up to my waist instantly. But, that's as far as I sunk.

Jay and I had not even noticed the place where the Canyon Crossing crew camped. We had stayed on river level and blew right by it. Camp was an old Tara homestead on a small rise above the river. The gringos slept in a very aromatic goat pen. The Taras slept on very rocky ground around the fire.

It wasn't the best campsite I have ever checked out in the comfort sense, but it was very interesting in all other regards. There were several swimming/bathing holes close by, as well as a hot spring pool that I had not noticed when I hiked through with Jay. From what I gathered, Skip had permission from the owner of the shack we were camped by to use the place.

There's a wonderful old *metate* — a big carved stone used for grinding corn — next to the shack. Since Skip's last Canyon Crossing trip, a couple of weeks before, this *metate* has been broken. Skip is near distraught, wondering if somehow he is responsible, wondering if his trips into the deepest recesses of Tarahumara-land aren't already resulting in negative impact. *Metates* are important to Tara life. They are hard to make, hard to come by and hard to live without. They are also, it would seem, hard to break, because these things are usually near-bouts 75-pound pieces of solid rock.

Our plan was to be on the trail before first light the next day because, not only did we have to climb all the way out of Tararecua — an elevation gain near-equal to climbing out of Copper Canyon itself — before lunch, but we would have to climb back down into a major side canyon of the Urique in the late afternoon.

We hurriedly breakfasted on day-old tortillas and fruit. This did not set so well with several of the Taras, who wanted eggs and cheese, like yesterday's breakfast. Skip came over and

Gary Michaels hikes out of Tararecua Canyon.

warned me that we might be facing a strike.

The trail out of Tararecua started directly across the river from camp. It was badly overgrown and the going was slow — too slow for many of the Tara porters who went up and around us.

By mid-morning, we had reached a level several hundred feet below the rim, at the top of the arroyo. This is where Skip ascertains how his group is doing. If folks are getting a tad tuckered from their time on the trail, he will bug out at this point — heading directly up to the rim. From there, he will hike out towards San Luis, meaning there are no more ascents or descents. We decided unanimously not to bug out. Everyone was feeling pretty good, even those members of the group who were not accustomed to desert travel.

We passed two springs, one of which was a carved log placed strategically below a dripping cave ceiling. This place was almost jungle-like lush.

The trail, which, by this time, was wide and well-graded, stayed level for the next few miles as we skirted around a few ridge fingers. We stopped for lunch at a point with a wonderful view of the deepest part of Copper Canyon. We could see miles up the Urique, just above where it makes its great bend.

Lunch consisted of one piece of battered fruit each, which

didn't bother the gringos one bit, as in our eyes, we had been gorging ourselves to this point. But, several of the Taras, especially the poor guy who was stuck with my community-utilized pack, decided they had had enough. Skip had to do some heavy politicking to keep them from dropping our gear and heading back to Sitagochi. Even after he mollified them with promises of near-future feasts, there was concern that they might, at any point, simply drop their loads in the middle of the trail and head home. This considered, we tried to keep the entire entourage in sight. That way, if our stuff was indeed dumped, we would at least know it.

This stretch of trail is among the most beautiful in all of Copper Canyon Country. The whole time, we maintained views of three of the best canyons around — Copper, Tararecua and Urique. As well, by mid-afternoon, the huge side canyon into which we would descend came into view. It was almost sensory overload. Our goal was a small homestead that sported such a fine orchard, it was known as the "Place with the Orange Trees."

The descent was steep and hot. As we cruised down, I recognized this side canyon as Arroyo Rurahuachi, the one just upriver from the arroyo I use to get from Divisadero to the Urique. I had twice been to the place where Arroyo Rurahuachi enters the Urique.

Only a trickle of water flows into the Urique from Arroyo Rurahuachi, but our camp was several miles up, where a nice little creek was flowing through a tight, multi-thousand-foot notch of a canyon. Great place.

The triathlete and the real estate agent each picked sleeping places down near the creek. Most of the group opted to sleep in the thick, seed-bearing weeds near our fire ring. Gay and I hopped over a stone fence into an orange grove. We laid out our groundcloth next to a small, hand-dug irrigation ditch. We strolled down to the creek for a bath. On the way, we passed well-tended rows of chiles, squashes, corn, beans and lemon and orange trees. The Tara owner of this spread, who was not at home, has himself a nice spot.

Dinner was indeed a feast. Since this was our last night, everything not yet on the road to digestion was fair game for consumption. We had eggs, tortillas, cheese, guacamole, oranges and tuna salad.

The five chickens, which had been carried all the way from Cusarare, made their way to meet the poultry Buddha, though they weren't on the evening menu. They would be roasted slowly over the fire all night. Then, they would be distributed to all carnivores for breakfast.

Skip and I stayed up talking about the future of Tarahumara-land. Both of us agreed that there is, without near-drastic action, scant chance for the Taras to maintain their near-pure cultural integrity for much longer. The main culprit is the Mexican logging industry. Since Taras tend to be laborers rather than entrepreneurs when they enter the money economy, they have prices set for them by outsiders — in this case, Mexicans. The Taras often end up working for less than minimum wage, while, essentially, giving their timber away.

Skip thinks that, in order for the Tara culture to survive reasonably intact, they need to get better control of their economic destiny. He believes that one way to usher that in is to establish a series of primitive backcountry lodging facilities, owned and operated by the Taras. The plan would be for Skip to help the Taras set these things up with financial, logistic, marketing and training help. Then, the Taras would take over.

These lodging facilities would be little more than hand-hewn cabins with small, community eating areas. Taras would do the cooking. Gringo backpackers would pay money to stay at these places. The Taras would then be relying less on their timber resources and, consequently, less on Mexicans who are trying to screw them economically.

Skip considers himself important to the actualization of this plan because he has the interest and the drive to get the ball rolling. He has connections with the local political and economic power structures, he has experience in running a lodging facility in Tarahumara-land, and he has the fiscal means which with to stake the initial stages of the project.

It's even within the realm of possibility that one day gringos will only be allowed to hike on certain trails and to sleep at these small lodges. Though this sounds like another case of over-gentrification of a land that is being touted in this book as interesting mainly because of its primitiveness, we must remember that the main thing here is the preservation of the Tara culture. This system would be no different, on the operational level, than the hut systems in the White Mountains of New Hampshire. And, though hiking hut-to-hut is not most people's idea of a wilderness experience, there are no indigenous cultures with a stake in the matter up in New Hampshire.

Too often places are ruined by overuse before anything is done to stabilize the situation. Though I haven't yet decided whether I agree with all or part of Skip's vision, I do respect the fact that someone is at least thinking about protecting Tarahumara-land before it gets Vibram-soled to death.

Once again, we were up well before dawn. As Gay and I sat on our groundcloth packing our packs, she turned to me and called me several names for spilling the water that she was sitting in. I politely informed her that I had not spilled any water. Then why was she sitting in something wet? she asked. I don't know. Look. She did.

She was sitting in a pool of blood. She had parked her posterior dead-smack on a blood-sucking Mexican bedbug — a cousin of the assassin bug. This little hoser had apparently had a gringo feast because, though bedbugs are only about an inch long, Gay was sitting in the A-positive equivalent of the Red Sea.

She focused her scientific self on the scene and summed up her feelings dispassionately and succinctly: "Gross," I believe, was the word she used. Before we completed our packing, we killed two other blood-gorged bedbugs on our groundcloth.

The plan this day was to hump it straight up to Divisadero. We would stop for a quick and light lunch only, because we wanted to catch the second-class train for Creel by 2:00 p.m.

This marked the third time that I had hiked out of the deep canyons to Divisadero. The previous two were marked by degrees of fatigue that did not go away for some days. This time, I hardly felt like I'd been hiking — except for the fact that I'd been wearing the same underwear for almost a week. The fact that we hadn't carried packs smeared a whole different veneer on the trip. Though I will never forget the weird feeling of photographing someone else with my pack on their back, it was okay. I don't feel comfortable hiring bearers and probably never will. And I don't feel entirely comfortable with the concept of someone else

The Canyon Crossing Crew last morning of trip.
Skip McWilliams (center), with hair slicked back, is helping
to tear breakfast — chicken — apart, and Jesus Olivas —
the "Mexican Gandolf" — is second from the left.

pointing the way and saying when it's time to eat supper. But, all in all, it was a great experience. We followed a route that I would have otherwise known about. And we got to meet some good people.

I recommend the concept of a guided trip in general and Skip McWilliams' Canyon Crossing in particular. An integral part of that recommendation stems from my hope that, should you decide to take Skip's trip — or any guided trip — you would return to Copper Canyon Country, the next time, on your own.

PARTICULARS

Cusarare To Divisadero

If you intend to try this route without a guide, you will need the Creel and San Jose Guacayvo 1:50,000 topos.

Since I have agreed to not be specific about describing this route, you'll have to go with this. Hire a Tara guide at Cusarare to Basirecota Hot Springs — only about three hours of hiking. From there, climb the ridge that separates Cusarare Canyon from Tararecua Canyon. Follow this ridge down towards the Urique — a full day's easy, level hike from Basirecota.

Towards the last arroyo in Tararecua Canyon before it enters the Urique, start heading down to the Rio San Ignacio in the bottom of Tararecua Canyon. Cross the river and head up to the opposite rim. Cross the ridge between Tararecua Canyon and the first downriver arroyo past the great bend of the Urique. Descend into this arroyo. Ascend the other side and point it towards Divisadero.

Because these directions are so vague, it may seem like it would be impossible to follow this route in even a half-assed fashion. If you are in good shape and know how to use a map and compass, you can do this. Just remember, don't define "success" during your trip by whether or not you achieve your geographic goal. If you find you need to turn around, or bug out on some alternate route, do so without hesitation. It takes a long time to learn the ins and outs of backcountry route-finding in Tarahumara-land. But no more so than any other geo-physically demanding area.

This route alternates between high country and deep canyon camping. Therefore, November to February are the best months. Remember, though, it will be cold up high this time of year.

You may pass some Tara orchards on this trip. Just remember that a Tara family is economically relying on that fruit for survival. If you want oranges, the Taras will be happy to sell them to you.

◄►

The trough spring near Tararecua Canyon,
where we froze our tails off.

9

San Luis (Magimachi) To Tararecua Canyon

So, here we are — four of us crammed into the bucket-seats of my Toyota pick-up, after what was supposed to be a 90-minute drive, that has ended up being three-and-a-half gut-jostling hours — when, before I've even turned off the engine, up comes running this toothless Tarahumara man who seems to be on the verge of a stuttering rage.

We're parked about 50 yards from the mission at San Luis, about five miles south of the road connecting Creel with Divisadero and about halfway between the two, south of Pitorreal. There's a fiesta going full-tilt, and we've decided to check it out. There are literally hundreds of Taras hanging out near the mission, including several million children, 900,000 of whom immediately descend on us in hopes that we have several tons of candy in our possession.

We get the impression right off that San Luis is not exactly on the normal tourist circuit — despite its proximity to the Chihuahua-Pacific Railroad. People are looking at us like we must have taken a major-league wrong turn somewhere near Mazatlán.

The toothless Tara man, who is not speaking any language I have ever heard, is jumping up and down shaking his head and pointing up a dirt jeep track — the extension of the one we have been following — then pointing to my truck, all the time jabbering on and on.

Finally, Juan, our Tarahumara guide — yes, the same Juan who went with us from Divisadero to Pamachi (Chapter 6) — steps in and plays the part of translator, though he is speaking Spanish. Ends up the man, likewise, has been babbling in Spanish, though his dental problems prevented me from even slightly understanding what in the world he was talking about.

Juan said that the man, who was the mayor of San Luis, was happy to have us there, but would we be so kind as to move our truck a few feet. Seems we were parked right in the middle of a *rarahipa* course. *Rarahipa* is the Tarahumara national game. And a bizarre game it is. It is usually played among four to eight teams, each of which can have from four to eight male members. These teams often represent particular villages and/or *ranchitos*, so there's a lot of local pride at stake. This pride is often manifested by side-betting.

The Taras are among the most notorious — though maybe that's too negative a word — gamblers in the world. They will bet everything they own — except their land and family — on not only *rarahipa*, but also on other, less formalized forms of competition, including quoits and stone throwing.

The Taras find recreation not so much in the betting itself, but from winning those bets. Therefore, even non-team members take an active roll in *rarahipas*. For two or three days before the event, they help in team preparation. Non-participants massage the contestants' legs, feed them corn beer and peyote, and give them pep talks. Of course, at the same time, these non-contestants are also drinking corn beer and eating peyote themselves.

But, this is not the most interesting aspect of pre-*rarahipa* preparations. Though the Taras profess to be Catholic, they also cling to many of their traditional animist beliefs. They believe in, and practice, magic. So, much time before and during *rarahipas* is spent laying curses on the other teams. Concurrently, much time is spent warding off the other teams' curses. The non-victorious teams do not look upon themselves as losers in an athletic competition sense. They consider that they were simply out-hexed.

I jumped in the truck and moved it 50 feet. The mayor came over, shook my hand and thanked me profusely. Several minutes later, the team that held the lead came running by. *Rarahipa* is a cross between kick-ball and a relay race played on a course that varies in length between 12 and 26 miles. Most fiesta-centered *rarahipas* go on for about three days, which is how long this one will last. We are on the scene about mid-way through the first day, meaning the runners — *corredores* — have been cruising already for about 12 hours.

The balls — *bollas*, which you can buy at the Tara Mission Store in Creel — are carved out of wood. They are about the size of a baseball. As each of the team members moves along the course, one runner will pass the ball ahead to the next. The ball is not actually kicked, because the Taras wear toe-less *huaraches* during *rarahipas*. Bare toes impacting solid wood for three straight days could have adverse physiological effects. So, they scoot the ball on top of their passing foot and fling it ahead.

At no time can the ball be carried. Each runner totes a stick, which he uses to displace the ball if it gets stuck under something — like a gringo truck. We're not certain what *rarahipa* rules say about 20th-century mechanical obstacles in the middle of the course, but, given the Taras' propensity for tossing random hexes around, we've glad we don't have the opportunity to find out. Referees are stationed all along the course and officiating is tight. Participants are allowed to rest, but they must make up any laps they miss before they're allowed to touch the ball again.

Although the runners who pass us by have put in at least 20 miles in very tough terrain, they aren't so much as sweating or breathing hard. One stops for a swig of water, but that's the only concession to fatigue we see. The contestants are carrying on a conversation like they're sitting around a poker table rather than hoofing it for several days through Copper Canyon Country.

Our plan is to drive out to a point overlooking the Urique River tonight, before hiking to the west rim of Tararecua Canyon in the morning. Unfortunately, the only way we can get to that point is to drive down the middle of the *rarahipa* course, the manners equivalent to a bunch of Taras running onto the court in the middle of a high school basketball game. We justify this by saying that we will drive off the side of the jeep track if we see any *corredores* approaching.

Juan, Gay, Gary Michaels — the real estate broker who was with us on our Canyon Crossing trip — and I hope to intersect Skip McWilliams' route (Chapter 8) at his "bug-out" point. We would like to camp near the spring where the water seeps from a cave ceiling into a carved log trough. Juan assures us that he knows exactly how to get there. He says he knows the neighborhood well, because his brother lives near San Luis.

At dawn, we drive back towards the road connecting Creel and Divisadero, which is very rough and only suitable for four-wheel-drive, high-clearance vehicles. Juan directs us to a small Tara homestead about three miles south of the Chihuahua-Pacific train tracks, where we will leave the truck unattended next to a corn field — something I hate doing. When I ask Juan if there's any danger of thievery or vandalism, he acts insulted. "No!" he answers emphatically, as though I have not only insulted him, but his entire tribe as well.

There was a well-worn trail from where we parked that headed up and over a small ridge. On top, we ran into two Tara men we had met the day before at the fiesta. They had been blatantly drunk then, and, apparently, they had not mended their ways in the interim. They were plowed and they wanted to chat. We were eager to be on our way, so we took our leave, which seemed to strike them as ill-mannered. Which was okay, except that they were heading in the direction of the truck. Great.

We descended several hundred feet into a small valley, where we passed several Tara homesteads, including that of Juan's brother. Juan asked us to wait while he ran over to give his regards. He returned a few minutes later, saying his sibling was not home.

Gary had been fighting a bad stomach, so we hiked very slowly. We estimated that it would take us about four or five hours to hike to the spring — maybe ten miles distant. This was some of the nicest hiking I have experienced in Copper Canyon Country. About a mile south of Juan's brother's, we started following an arroyo downhill. Though it was hot and sunny, there was plenty of shade. We passed several springs, but did not fill up because they looked too dirty. After two hours, the trail forked and we headed to the left, slightly uphill towards a ridge top. Again, the hiking was very easy, but something seemed, to me, directionally amiss. I had been trying to figure out exactly where we were in relation to Skip's Canyon Crossing route. This was atypically tough for Tarahumara-land because the woods had been very dense the whole time. Usually, there will be plenty of visual opportunities to check out the surrounding terrain. When we were hiking with Skip, he had pointed this route out to us from a distance of about five miles. Though I was unable to take good bearings, it just seemed that we were off-track.

When I mentioned this to Juan, he looked at me like I was the dumbest gringo ever to hoist a pack. He tactfully said something along the lines of how this was his territory so, perhaps, we'd all be better off if I kept my mixed-bearings to myself.

Ordinarily, I would have been more argumentative. But, when I stopped and thought about it, it really didn't matter where we were going. As long as we crossed paths with a water source by nightfall, everything was hunky-dory.

By the time the ridge broke out of the thick woods, I was positive Juan was taking us to the wrong spring (*fuente*). I had ascertained which of the adjoining arroyos were which and, as far as I could tell, we were at least two ridges too far west. Juan kept shaking his head. Gary and Gay had not even been trying to maintain their bearings because they figured Juan and I had matters well in-hand. Ha-ha.

After four hours on the trail, we passed a campsite that seemed to fit the description of the one Skip uses on his bug-out route. It was right next to the trail, spacious, perfectly flat, overlooking a deep arroyo, with a small spring nearby and plenty of wood. Had we any brains, we would have dropped our gear and ourselves right here. But, I had remembered a very nice campsite near the spring that was our goal. And, if Juan was leading us to a different spring, that was okay, too, because, he said, there was a nice place to camp there, too.

About half an hour later, the ridge got real skinny and we stepped out onto a small saddle. Then it all fell together. Juan, of course, had been correct all along. The ridge we had been traversing continued south until it became the point where we had stopped for lunch with Skip on the second-to-the-last day of his Canyon Crossing.

We dropped off the saddle to the east and began descending into the side canyon we had climbed out of Tararecua Canyon with Skip. At this point, the hike became less pleasant because there wasn't much of a trail. What trail there was sported prodigious amounts of loose rock. And it was very steep. We picked our way through the spiny brush and, an hour later, we intersected the Canyon Crossing route. Ten minutes after that, we were filling our water bottle at the trough spring. Some Tara, who knows who, who knows when, got a fairly good-sized tree trunk, carved out its innards and set it in this small cave, where water slowly drips out of the ceiling and fills it.

Though we were exactly where I was hoping we would be, we had a problem. I have been told over the years that too much beer will eventually cause your memory to erode like mud down a river. I thought I remembered a nice, flat, dry camping spot close to the spring. I must've been thinking about that time up who knows where, because there was nothing that even remotely fit that bill here. Gay and Gary both decided then and there not to buy this guidebook. We walked a short ways down the trail, following the Canyon Crossing route, until we reached a small point that was "only" at about an 89-degree slope — the flattest spot for miles. We placed our packs on the edge of a cliff with the idea that they would prevent us from rolling off during the night.

We gathered some wood and built a fire right in the middle of the trail because it was the only non-vertical place around. This section of trail is well-used, so we worried about the possibility of a burro train passing by. If that happened, we would have had to extinguish the flames because there was no other way around.

The views more than made up for our discomfort, however. When we had hiked out of Tararecua Canyon the week before, the light had been mid-day harsh. Now, it was sunset gentle. The shadows and tricks of canyon light were inter-playing with one of the deepest abysses in Tarahumara-land. And the vegetation surrounding us was more like Costa Rica than the rest of Copper Canyon Country. It was lush, cool and thick.

This was about the time we realized that the *rarahipa* spectators must have hexed us afterall. One of them had said, under his breath, something like, "Why don't you stupid gringos go where the sun don't shine." Which is exactly where we were. Our campsite, to the best of my knowledge, is the only place in this part of Mexico that is permanently in the shade. This is a great thing for all those times of the year that are not the dead of winter. We were here in, you guessed it, the dead of winter. It started getting cold fast. I had just brought a light sleeping bag because...hell, I don't know why.

Gay and Gary each had warm bags. Juan had only a couple of thin blankets. By 10:00 p.m., Juan and I were having a teeth-chattering contest. I was winning. I have never been so cold in my life. I moved over next to the fire. By midnight, my stylish bouffant was near-bouts one with the coals. Juan got up about 4:00 a.m. and stoked the fire to the degree that I awoke thinking I was an integral part of a holocaust, which didn't sound all that bad.

We were on the trail early — though we ascended towards the saddle by a different route. In most places in Tarahumara-land, you are usually rewarded if you spend a little extra time route-finding. Just uphill from the trough spring, a burro trail headed up. And it went all the way to the saddle. So, our hour-long near-miserable descent the day before was an exercise in stupidity.

Four hours later, we were eating Ritz crackers and peanut butter back at the truck. The owner of the field next to which we parked had returned home. He walked over to chat, holding the filthiest baby I have ever seen. But, the kid looked happy and well-fed.

Three hours later, we dropped Juan off in Creel. Unlike our rim-to-rim trip, we felt he had earned a good tip, if for no other reason than for putting up with my questioning of his route-finding abilities. He immediately ran off to buy a new pair of shoes — the first he had ever owned. I ran into him in Creel several days later. He was back to wearing his *huaraches* and his feet were sporting some serious-looking blisters.

PARTICULARS

San Luis (Magimachi) To Tararecua Canyon

You will need the 1:50,000 San Jose Guacayvo map, although the 1:250,000 San Juanito map might suffice.

This is a hard route to find, but it is worth the effort whether you want to just hike in and out, like we did, or whether you want to intersect one of the other routes in the vicinity.

Take the train to Pitorreal, a small Mexican town about halfway between Creel and Divisadero. There, you will need to hire a vehicle, which should be pretty easy. Just ask around. Tell the driver you want to go to San Luis. There are actually two places with this name — one being where the mission school is located, marked on the San Jose Guacayvo map as Internado San Luis, the other being the original *ranchito*, marked on the map only as Magimachi. Sort of confusing, but easily dealt with. Tell the driver you want to go to Magimachi. He will not be able to drive you all the way, but he will drop you off at the trailhead.

Hike over a small ridge, southeast towards the *ranchito* of Colurabo. From there, it will be a gradual downhill to Magimachi. Just south of Magimachi, you will meet a small arroyo that, depending on the season, may or may not have water in it. This arroyo is the east fork of the east fork of Arroyo Rurahuachi. The trail at this point will be well-traveled and easy to follow. Hike south for three kilometers (almost two miles). When you reach the obvious fork, bear left and stick to the west side of the ridge. This ridge heads south and you will stay with it for several more miles.

You pass a perfect campsite on your right. Just before it, there is a very small side canyon where you can find water by following it down towards the bottom of the arroyo.

Continue on down the ridge until you reach a small saddle. Cross over to the east side of the ridge here and look for a small burro trail. This will parallel the top of the ridge for a mile or so, before switch-backing down into the arroyo on your left. A mile more and you will run right into the trough spring. You can either camp a few hundred feet past the spring, or you can work your way down into Tararecua Canyon, which is east of you. There is a good campsite on the other side of the Rio San Ignacio. It should take two hours to reach the San Ignacio. From there, you can cross over to Cusarare, following in reverse the route described in Chapter 8.

Or, from the small saddle, you can descend into Arroyo Rurahuachi and make your way over to Divisadero.

If you choose to explore in this area, be aware that there are plenty of cliffs. Don't force a route that is not there.

Also, you could find yourself wandering close to Tara houses. Please be on your best manners here because these are people who have chosen to live way off the beaten path. We may all infer that they have chosen to do so because they like their privacy.

◄►

Gay at the Ventana near Basaseachi Falls.

Basaseachi Falls

H ere we take a short detour from Tarahumara-land proper. About a 140-kilometer (85-mile), four-hour, drive northwest of Creel is one of the highest waterfalls in North America — Basaseachi (bah sah SAY ah chee or bah sah say AH chee). While there is some disagreement as to exactly where 1,000-foot-high Basaseachi ranks — somewhere around the fourth highest in North America — suffice to say that this place is not to be missed, despite the fact that it is not conveniently located.

Like Cusarare Falls — indeed, like all waterfalls in the Sierra Madre — there is a big difference between rainy season and dry season water levels. Gay and I drove to Basaseachi from Creel on Thanksgiving Day 1988, understanding full well that we would not be witnessing Basaseachi at its most spectacular. But, since we had decided that we actually preferred Cusarare Falls at low water, perhaps such would be the case with Basaseachi, which is almost ten times as high as Cusarare.

The drive was interesting enough, in and of itself, to justify an 85-mile trip from the heart of Copper Canyon Country. And I'm not just talking about the splendid high-sierra scenery. Before we had been on the road an hour, we crossed a bridge at an unreasonable — in retrospect — rate of speed, maybe 45 miles per hour. This was no jeep track. We're talking about a fairly major dirt/gravel road that serves as the predominant transportation artery for several hundred square miles. Logging trucks by the dozen pass along it every day, as well as ordinary passenger cars.

So, I had 'er in fourth gear and was cruising along happily with a Tecate resting in my lap. Without warning, that Tecate became one with the atmosphere. We both found ourselves suspended in that uncomfortable nether region between the seats and the ceiling before, equally as suddenly, being replanted firmly back in our seats by at least nine "Gs".

A huge hole, about four feet deep, as wide as the entire road and 30 feet long had eroded on the north side of this bridge about ten miles northwest of San Juanito. We felt like we were in one of those Nissan commercials filmed in the middle of the Baja 1000. The truck flew through the air with the greatest of ease, landed in the middle of said mammoth hole, hit the "cliff" on the far side, flew through the air some more, before resuming its appointed rounds. Thankfully, nothing in the oil pan or spring regions was damaged. The remainder of the drive was smooth as silk, at least partially because we drove the rest of the way in second gear.

We arrived at the entrance to Basaseachi close to sunset. Unlike the mythical Copper Canyon National Park that is marked on some maps, Basaseachi National Park actually exists. There's an entrance sign, but no other facilities within the park boundaries worth mentioning, which is the way a national park ought to be. There is also a small Mexican town named Basaseachi, but, it is a few kilometers further down the road as you are driving from Creel. We opted to stop for a quick look at the falls before dark.

It's about a five-kilometer (three-mile) drive from the main road to the overlook parking lot, which is an interesting place in its own right. There's no notice that you have indeed reached the point where you shouldn't drive further. Neither are there guardrails. A miscue here would be attention grabbing because from that parking lot, you can spit directly into the beautiful river valley into which Basaseachi Falls plunges.

You may notice several feet of locked-brake tire marks ending about six inches from said drop off into said deep valley. Guess who?

We walked the few hundred feet to one of the overlooks — *divisaderos*. Although we had seen dozens of photos of Basaseachi, we were unprepared for its actual astounding geophysical grandeur. The falls themselves are on the opposite side of the valley. The late afternoon light was playing off the delicate ribbon of tumbling water, making rainbows that filled half the chasm beneath our feet. But the falls were just one — albeit the most significant one — of the things that make this place so beauteous. The whole valley, with some of the most-sheer cliffs in northern Mexico, is wonderful. The trees at the bottom were in the height of fall colors.

We wanted to stay at the overlook for hours, but since it was getting dark, we drove into the village of Basaseachi. There are several ways you can make quick judgments of small Mexican towns. One of the best is to find out if it is wet or dry — that is, is it legal to sell alcohol or not? If it is wet, you can pretty much assume that the town is reasonably mellow. If it is dry, there is a reason and, unlike some places in the American Deep South that are dry, that reason has nothing to do with religion. The Mexican government outlaws the sale of alcohol only if a town or region is particularly rough.

Basaseachi feels particularly rough, which is not surprising considering that it is the center of the logging industry in the northern Sierra Madre. Nothing against loggers, you understand. We pulled into the parking lot of the local pool hall to ask a few questions about the town. The six gentlemen who were standing out in front looked like some of the nastier characters from the movie "Papillon." We drove on at the first opportune moment. I really wished that I had not asked them about camping in the national park. They were all smiling as we drove away.

We considered getting a room for the night. On the west side of town is a little four-room hotel named the Alma Rosa. Since we were here during the off-season, the proprietor almost started jumping up and down when we pulled up. Unfortunately, for both of us, his rates were a little on the high side — about $15 U.S. a night. There was an American family of four staying there because their rental car had developed a crack in the oil pan on the road between Basaseachi and La Junta. They were stuck without wheels until the rental car folks sent a new vehicle from Chihuahua City, an event that was supposed to happen "soon." I wouldn't be surprised if they are there still.

There's another entrance to the park heading south from the middle of town. We drove down that road in the dark, hoping to run across a good field to camp in. Just past the park entrance, we passed a sign proclaiming a "Zona de Acampar" — campsites. We pulled in just as it started snowing. We celebrated Thanksgiving with spaghetti and tomato sauce — a nice change from our usual dried backpacking fare.

During the night, the wind started blowing heavy duty. The temperature dropped into the teens. By morning, the skies were steel gray and it was sleeting. We opted to drive back to the Alma Rosa for breakfast, where we had some of the best cheese enchiladas we have ever eaten, washed down by about 30 cups of hot coffee each.

It was nearing noon when we returned to the park. From the trailhead near the "Zona de Acampar," it's two kilometers to the closest overlook. Signs point the way. The trail, which has got to be one of the most heavily traveled in Mexico — though we were the only ones there this day — follows Basaseachi Creek, which sports some wild rock formations along its banks. After 30 minutes of very easy walking, we found ourselves staring over the edge of the falls. The overlook we had stopped at last night was several miles distant — giving the long-view perspective. Though breathtaking and all, we preferred this view because we could peer over the edge.

I climbed down to the lip of the falls, where the creek passes under a small rock arch before plummeting down to the valley below. It was awesome. If it had been the rainy season, the creek would have been too high for this kind of tomfoolery.

From the top of the falls, the trail crosses the creek, before heading up and over a small ridge to the east. Then it goes DOWN, 1,000 feet in half a mile. This is an aerobic experience to say the least — even on the downhill. Some poor soul actually carried enough sacks of concrete down here to make several hundred steps. A nice thought, but not very convenient because they lock you into a pre-measured step length.

Ten minutes from the bottom, there's a *ventana* — a figurative "window." This is the place where many of the published photos of Basaseachi are taken. For good reason. Because it was well past rainy season and because it was so windy, the tiny stream of water that comprised this superlative natural phenomenon was whipping back and forth across the cliff face like a cat flicking its tail. When the wind really kicked up, there was no water at

The small arch above oblivion.

all, only cold mist, most of which evaporated before hitting the valley floor.

At the bottom of the falls is another of those lovely pools that, were it not for the cold weather, would have made for some wonderful swimming. A trail leads from the pool downriver into the heart of Basaseachi Canyon. We wanted to follow it down a few miles, but the weather was getting even worse. So, we humped back up to the top, which took quite a while. Although this is a short hike, it is very strenuous.

We climbed around on the rocks upriver from the falls for a few hours and were as captivated by these rock formations as with the falls themselves.

On the way back to Creel, we passed an old beater of a Toyota truck that was broken down on the side of the road. There were four people, none of whom had coats, standing around the open hood looking very bummed. The fan belt was broken and, though I always carry a spare, it was the wrong size for this corroded relic.

The owner of the truck was a physician named Victorio. We gave Victorio a ride into the small village of Yoquivo. He told us that he took care of three public clinics in this region, each of which was 50 miles from the next health care facility. All graduates of Mexican medical schools are required by law to spend one year working in the boondocks. He told us that the government paid him barely enough money to survive. As well, his budget for supplies and medicine was almost non-existent. Yet, he had become so attached to this part of Mexico that he was considering signing up for another year. He knew he could make more money elsewhere, but, he said, there was no place else where he could do as much social good.

We dropped Victorio off at the clinic/home of another public health doctor, who heartily loaded us up with tostadas, tequila and thanks. We were told that Americans don't have the reputation for stopping to lend assistance. Though I don't agree with that observation, it's always good to know that you've played a small part in remedying a misconception about one's people.

▐▄▀▄▐▀▄▐▀▄▐▀▄▐▀▄▌ PARTICULARS ▐▀▄▐▀▄▐▀▄▐▀▄▐▀▄▌

Basaseachi Falls

I haven't had any luck obtaining a topo of this area, though you really shouldn't need one. Dr. Robert Schmidt's map, available at the Tarahumara Mission Store in Creel, covers Basaseachi sufficiently.

Because it is about 140 kilometers from Creel, Basaseachi is somewhat difficult to get to, although you don't want to visit Tarahumara-land without checking it out. There are three roads to Basaseachi, but no bus service that I know of. (You might want to ask at the bus station in Chihuahua City.) The road from La Junta — one of the train stops between Chihuahua City and Creel — is paved just about the entire 80-kilometer distance. The 100-kilometer road from San Juanito is not paved, but it is in very good shape. Each of these roads see enough traffic that you could try hitching. There is also a very rough road from the western city of Ciudad Obregon.

Both Margarita's Guest House and the Parador in Creel offer tours to Basaseachi, but they can be expensive. You would want to get together with as many people as possible to offset the cost. The problem with these tours is that they last but one day. So, you're looking at eight hours on the road in order to experience Basaseachi for only about four hours. The driver will be glad to stay over for a night, but that means you will be paying for an extra day's use of the vehicle, as well as the driver's meals and lodging.

Sunracer Tours, out of Tucson, Arizona, listed in the "Nuts & Bolts" chapter, offers tours to Basaseachi.

If you are driving, gas is available in the town of Basaseachi. There are also several small stores there, but don't count on being able to buy very much in the way of food. Don't forget to try the enchiladas at the Alma Rosa, and beware the poison oak along the trail from the top of the falls to the valley.

◄►

Dean Fairburn near the Urique River just downriver from the Incised Meanders. Photo by Robert Gedekoh.

11

Umira Bridge To The Incised Meanders Of The Urique River

By Robert Gedekoh

Not far from the tiny village of Umira — sometimes spelled "Humira" — the Urique River flows through a deep, serpentine cleft in the Sierra Madre. Commonly referred to as the "Incised Meanders," this magnificent portion of Mexico's Barranca del Cobre provides a unique backpacking opportunity.

The canyon is visually stunning. Sheer cliffs plummet 1,500 feet to the very edge of the river. Towering pines cling to the rock walls, their size dwarfed by the scale of the canyon. The emerald Urique flows over, under and through gigantic boulder fields and topples over falls. The river has sculpted its bed, leaving behind what must surely be some of the most-inviting swimming holes in the world.

Such a magnificent area does not, of course, come without a steep price of admission. Access to the canyon is difficult, to say the least. The Samachique topo map does not show any trails into the Incised Meanders, and we spent most of our four days in the canyon bushwhacking, bouldering along the river bed, wading in waist-deep cold water and scaling cliffs. Only on rare occasions did we stumble across any semblance of a path.

The canyon is extremely remote. We encountered no one during our exploration and there was little evidence that the canyon is visited often, either by locals or by other backpackers.

When we entered the canyon, we knew we were on our own. There would be no rangers or mountain rescue teams ready to extricate us in the event of catastrophe. That sense of adventure is an integral part of the allure of backpacking in this part of Mexico, and those unwilling or unable to accept responsibility for themselves would do well to choose another destination. The risks of exploring this canyon are real. One of our party had a close encounter with a rattlesnake. We traversed several narrow ledges hundreds of feet in the air. And many of the boulders along the river were extremely slippery, providing countless opportunities for devastating orthopedic injuries.

We identified three ways to descend to the Incised Meanders. One could park at the bridge, about two miles south of Umira, and follow the riverbed. We did not choose this route because we were unable to locate anyone there to watch our pick-up truck while we were gone. We also noted that the riverbed downstream from the bridge was narrow with steep walls. Passage would have been possible, but difficult.

A better point of access lies about a mile up the road towards Umira. The road is cut into the mountainside here, and it is possible to look down into the canyon at the walls of the Incised Meanders. To reach the river, one must traverse or skirt a long talus slide into a dry arroyo. Beware the loose rock on the initial steep slope. It would be easy to trigger a small rock slide. From the floor of the arroyo, there is a primitive path to the Urique. We used this route to exit the canyon. This point of access brings the explorer to the river about a mile upstream of the first major meander. It is easy walking downriver to the heart of the Meanders.

A more difficult, but decidedly more interesting way to enter the canyon is down the Arroyo Umira. We parked our truck at

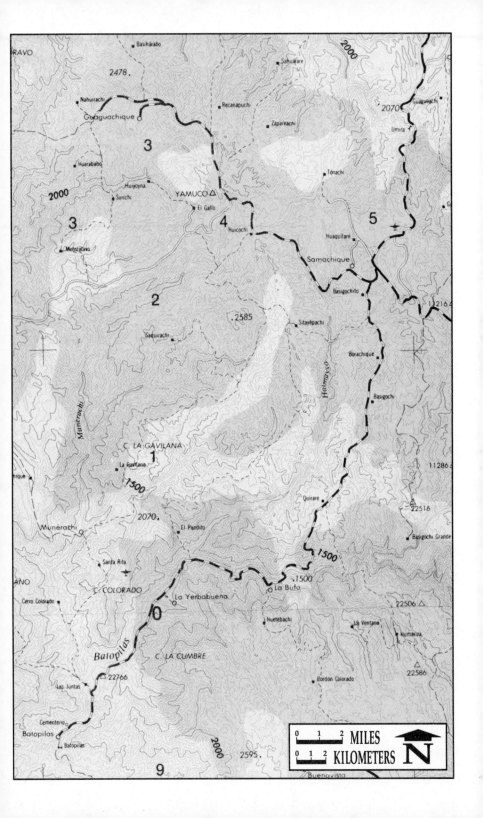

one of the *ranchitos* in Umira, the family graciously agreeing to protect our vehicle during our trek for 10,000 pesos.

Then we hiked along the stream that flows from the village through a large apple orchard and several corn fields. A number of Tarahumara families live in primitive houses along the hillside and they laughed exuberantly as we strolled by, no doubt speculating on the misadventures likely to befall the gringos in the wild canyon below.

Eventually, the stream entered a forested area and the gradient increased dramatically, cutting into the plateau. Precipitous slopes and walls appeared on both sides of the stream and it was necessary to boulder from side to side to continue on. At some locations the stream became so congested by rockfall that it was advantageous to trek a hundred or so feet above the level of the water.

Finally, after we had covered about three miles, the stream tumbled precipitously down a massive rock jumble. From our vantage point atop a 20-foot falls, we could see that the stream was about to make a plunge of at least 500 feet to the main canyon below. The streambed was clearly impassable without ropes and rock climbing expertise, and the cliffs on either side suggested that we had reached a dead end.

We set up camp on a tiny sand bar just above the falls, convinced that we would have to make the rigorous climb back up the arroyo the next day. Our surroundings were exquisite, but we were frustrated by our impasse.

My friend, Mike Bush, decided to climb the cliff on the right side of the arroyo, facing downstream, to take photographic advantage of the evening light. It was there that he found himself seated less than a foot from a six-foot coiled rattlesnake, which, fortunately, seemed more nonplussed than alarmed by the intruder.

I spotted a ledge on the cliff across the stream which looked like it also offered a promising view, so I scaled the wall, knees trembling a bit more with each step. When I reached the sanctuary of a ledge about 60 feet above the streambed, I was surprised to discover the hint of a path that cut across the canyon wall to the main canyon. I followed this "trail" warily, hanging onto trees and vegetation for support and traversing one five-inch-wide ledge above a 30-foot drop.

The path continued onto the very brink of a sheer rock wall, 700 feet above the Urique. And so, in the midst of an attack of vertigo, I got my first breathtaking look into the bowels of Copper Canyon. The last rays of the evening sun cast eerie shadows and several maples, far below along the river, blazed orange and yellow and red in response to the changing season.

After several minutes, I made a second startling discovery. A ledge cornered the angled-face of the cliff, giving way to a direct, albeit hair-raising, descent to the river. I returned to camp ecstatic that we would be spared the need to backtrack to the road.

The next morning, my compadres followed me into the canyon. Mike, who used to hang utility lines for a living, had no problems with the route, but Dean Fairburn and I, neither of us very fond of heights, found crossing the ledges with 30 pounds on our backs more than a little unnerving. Some climber's webbing, a 50-foot piece of rope and a few carabiners, and the knowledge of how to use them, would have come in handy.

We made our next camp at the base of the arroyo on a large sandy beach. Then we bouldered our way about four miles downstream to a point beyond which the riverbed seemed impassable without climbing gear. We returned to camp about dusk, built a campfire and settled in for the night. A full moon rose above the canyon walls. It was so bright, we didn't need flashlights. We watched the bats fly out of the caves carved into a cliff across the river and listened to the Urique gurgle past the rocks upstream.

The following day, we donned our packs and headed upriver. The going was tough for several miles. We bouldered across the river several times to circumvent rock walls. Other times we crawled through tunnels under the gigantic rocks that had tumbled into the canyon. Thick clumps of bamboo grow along the river and cactus seem to take root in profusion where handholds are needed most.

Being ardent kayakers, we evaluated the Urique as a potential run. All agreed that it would be a technical nightmare. The river flows under rocks as much as around them. At high water, the river would be ripe with undercuts and siphons. And portaging would be a logistical horror show.

After four miles, we approached the Incised Meanders and the river assumed a serpentine course. Fortunately, the boulder fields became less intimidating and we started to make better time. But it was necessary to wade the river six times because of the canyon walls. We hoisted our packs above our heads as we passed through chest-deep water.

We made camp that night in the middle of the Meanders, about a quarter-mile above a river-wide 15-foot falls. We spotted large cat tracks along the river and concluded that they had probably been left by a bobcat, which are indigenous to the area. We slept again under the full moon.

The next morning, we continued upriver — about one and one-half more miles — until we reached the dry arroyo mentioned previously as an alternate point of access. Within an hour, we arrived at the road and I quickly hiked to Umira and retrieved the truck.

The Incised Meanders offers a spectacular wilderness experience to those adequately prepared to meet the challenge. This is clearly no place for carelessness. Rescue from the canyon would be difficult, if not impossible. Some climbing gear and experience might prove useful.

Clumsy individuals prone to falls and those inadequately outfitted should not attempt this trek, especially the descent down Arroyo Umira, which is particularly perilous.

As always, low-impact camping must be the rule. The canyon is free of debris, fire rings, etc. It deserves to stay that way.

Robert Gedekoh M.D. is a regional editor for American Whitewater. He has written for River Runner, American Whitewater and the Pittsburgh Press. He lives in Elizabeth, Pennsylvania.

▛▞▚▞▚▞▚▞▚ | PARTICULARS | ▛▞▚▞▚▞▚▞▚

Umira Bridge To The Incised Meanders Of The Urique River

You will need the 1:50,000 Samachique topo.

Access to Umira Bridge may be somewhat inconvenient. It is about halfway between Creel and Batopilas, which is a long way to hitchhike, although I talked to three people who did so and said they caught rides easily.

You may want to hop the every-other-day bus from Creel to Batopilas. Just ask the driver to let you off at Umira.

If you have your own vehicle, the road to Umira is good. The drive from Creel should take about two or three hours, depending on how often you stop to ogle at the scenery.

There is a very small store in Umira.

◄►

*View of Batopilas Canyon from the road
connecting Creel and Batopilas.*

12

Batopilas

If there is one piece of civilization in Tarahumara-land worth visiting, it's the wonderfully weird town of Batopilas. Founded in 1632, Batopilas was once one of Mexico's richest towns, owing to the silver ore in the area. Several of the buildings constructed during the apex of that affluence now lie in examinable ruins, providing visitors with a rare chance to view very old non-mission architecture.

Until the late 1970s, there wasn't even a road to Batopilas. You could drive only as far as La Bufa, which, despite its prominence on some maps, consists of nothing more than a few houses. From there, it was five or six hours more on foot on the ancient Camino Real, a trail that follows the lovely Rio Batopilas. As well, the town was electrified only in late 1988, after a failed attempt to do so in 1983. Many of the buildings there have had private generators for years, but that was it.

Batopilas is no *ranchito*. It is, rather, home to several thousand people. It has a large church, several hotels, several schools and plenty of European-feeling curvy back alleys.

The road connecting Creel with Batopilas is a major-league engineering marvel. It is about 150 kilometers (94 miles) long, only the first 40 of which were paved as of late 1988. The trip from Creel, which takes a minimum of five hours, will be one of the highlights of your visit to Tarahumara-land, whether you drive it yourself or take the thrice-weekly bus. The road passes through high sierra topography, punctuated by spectacular rock formations and cliff faces. It goes through several towns, most notably, Quirare. And it crosses the Rio Urique at Umira Bridge — the upper reaches of Copper Canyon itself.

But, all of that is small potatoes compared to the descent from the high country into Batopilas Canyon. A few miles south of Quirare, the view of the almost 6,000-foot deep (1850 meters) abyss, which is one of the most breathtaking in all of Copper Canyon Country, opens up. And, what you see is what you get — the road heads right on down. In the next ten miles — 16 kilometers — there are over 200 curves and almost 20 major switchbacks. After that, the road crosses the Rio Batopilas.

Then, the *real* fun begins. The tendency, once you've completed the big descent, is to think that Batopilas is right around the next bend. Wrong. It's at least another hair-raising hour's drive downriver. This is my favorite part of the drive, though it is also the most dangerous because, every inch of the way, there's a major dropoff on the right-hand side as you're heading towards Batopilas. On the opposite side of the river, you can easily see the Camino Real, which is still used by locals — Tarahumaras and Mexicans — leading burro trains.

Batopilas is located on the west bank of the Rio Batopilas in one of the deepest and most arid canyons in Tarahumara-land. It was built between the river and the canyon walls. Thus, Batopilas is several miles long, but only a few blocks wide — at the most. In many places, it is only one block wide.

Batopilas is right in the middle of Copper Canyon Country's tropical fruit-producing region. Flowers bloom here year-round, lending a coastal, Central American feel to the town. But, this place is anything but coastal. Though the river runs a stone's throw from every building in town, Batopilas is in the middle of a cactus-adorned section of desert that makes Tucson seem mild by comparison. The highest temperature ever recorded in these parts — 112 degrees F; 44.5 degrees C — was measured right in beautiful downtown Batopilas. Thus, I recommend visiting this area in the dead of winter. And not just because of the temperatures. Summertime insects here can be numerous and voracious.

Batopilas is also one of the center for drug cultivation and transportation in the Sierra Madre. This, combined with its isolation, gives Batopilas an air of the wild West, Sierra Madre style. You will see men walking around with pistols stuck in their belts and no-nonsense looks in their eyes. Surprisingly, or maybe not

Burros near Rio Batopilas just downriver from Batopilas.

so surprisingly, Batopilas is a "dry" town — there are no saloons.
If you want to wet your whistle here, you need to bring your own.

You will likely venture into Batopilas because it is the gateway
to some of Tarahumara-land's most appealing backpacking. But
you would be making a mistake if you did not spend at least a
full day exploring the town. Most of Batopilas' buildings were
built in the early 20th century, but there are many ruins from
the 17th and 18th centuries — to say nothing of the fact that
even those "new" 20th century edifices look like they're as old
as the hills. Especially interesting is the ruin of the Hacienda de
San Miguel, located on the east side of the river just before the
bridge, as you are coming into town. This building served as
the residence of one of the area's first silver tycoons, Alexander
Shepard. It also served as the office for the local mining company.

Batopilas is also highly recommended for just hanging out and
reading. It is a relaxing little town. The perfect place to put your
feet up after your hiking trip into the backcountry of Tarahumara-
land.

▰▱▰▱▰▱▰▱▰▱ PARTICULARS ▰▱▰▱▰▱▰▱▰▱

Batopilas

There are busses connecting Creel with Batopilas, leaving from the plaza in Creel at 7:00 a.m., Tuesdays, Thursdays and Saturdays. The trip can take as long as ten hours. The busses make the return trip to Creel at 4:00 a.m. on Mondays, Wednesdays and Fridays. Fare is about $10 U.S. Be sure to verify times and schedules. You would be well-advised to pack a lunch and water bottle for the drive.

Also, Margarita's, the Parador and the Hotel Nuevo in Creel all offer guided tours to Batopilas, as does the Copper Canyon Lodge in Cusarare.

There are at least three lodging facilities in Batopilas, with another getting ready to open in late 1989. The Batopilas branch of the Parador is located right across the street from the church. Private rooms cost about $10 U.S. a night. Room cost is the same for one or two people. There are three clean communal baths with hot water. The Hotel Batopilas is located about three blocks north of the plaza. Rooms are rented for $5 per person, no matter how many people share a room. Sports one bathroom that is kept in a barely acceptable state of cleanliness. Bustillo's is located right on the east side of the plaza. This place is run by an English-speaking woman, who also deals in Tarahumara artifacts. She sells some of the nicest pots in the area. Cost is $5 U.S. per person with communal bath. Suzanne McWilliams and Skip McWilliams, owners of the Copper Canyon Lodge, purchased a building, which they have named La Hacienda at Batopilas, in early 1989 that they plan on converting into a hotel. Call 1-800-521-1455 for details.

There are several places to eat in Batopilas, most notably Michaela's, which is south of the plaza on a winding side street. You should ask directions. Micha, as she is known, serves meals in her house at a cost of 6,000 pesos per person, including one soft drink. You pretty much get served whatever she has on hand, though the portions are always hearty. The Hotel Batopilas also has a family-run restaurant.

There are several small grocery stores in town. All of them sell cheap fresh fruit, which Batopilas is famous for. You can also buy gas here most of the time.

Though it is tempting to explore the area surrounding Batopilas in great detail, you would be well-advised to stick to the main tourist routes, which are detailed in the following two chapters. If there is any place in Copper Canyon Country where you can find yourself stumbling into a marijuana field, the Batopilas area is it. If you do not stray far from the beaten path, you have nothing to worry about. Despite its drug roots, Batopilas is a very laid-back place. You may, however, be approached to buy drugs. Just say "no!" Also, be prepared for military check-points on the road between Creel and Batopilas.

◄►

Suspension bridge over Rio Batopilas just upriver from Satevo Mission.

Batopilas To Satevo Mission

At any moment, I expect Alfred Hitchcock to walk around the corner, the look on his face betraying the fact that even he feels spooked. This place — Satevo Mission, two very easy walking hours downriver from Batopilas — puts the Bates Mansion to shame when it comes to potential horror quotient. If a bunch of your buddies got you so drunk that you passed out near-dead, then carted your inebriated carcass to Satevo and placed you on the altar on a moonlit night, your psyche would never recover. You would wake up and, once you checked out your surroundings, that would be that with regards your sanity. You would run screaming into the dark Mexican night, badly bent forevermore.

The wide, level trail from Batopilas to Satevo provides the best day-hike in Tarahumara-land. Not only is the hiking as easy as it gets, but the scenery is unparalleled. This is the heart of Batopilas Canyon, the walls of which rise almost 2,300 meters — 7,400 feet — straight up to the high sierra, dotted the whole way by huge Organ Pipe cactuses. At the same time, the Rio Batopilas is making an argument for being the most attractive river in Copper Canyon Country.

But the walk takes a backseat to the destination — Satevo Mission. The history of this mission has been lost. No one knows for certain when it was built, or by whom. According to local sources, it is older than Batopilas, meaning it was built in the very early 1600s. About the same time as Jamestown, Virginia.

More intriguing than the "when?" or "by whom?" of Satevo Mission's history is the "why?" Satevo Mission is a very large worship facility by local standards. The area has never had a population large enough to justify a hallowed edifice of these proportions.

Thus, why on earth would anyone — almost certainly a Jesuit — feel a need to come into the wilderness to build such a monstrosity? It must have taken years to complete. And, the work must have required the services of scores of Tarahumaras. They dedicated what surely must have been years of their lives to make Satevo Mission a physical reality. Why? Surely they didn't fall for the Jesuits' mythology...

No matter the fabric of its history. Satevo Mission is a day-hiking destination to beat all day-hiking destinations. Located in a particularly arid, half-mile-wide stretch of flood plain along the Rio Batopilas, Satevo Mission is the centerpiece of a small Mexican community of the same name. The mission itself has three domes and a belltower several stories high. Like most backcountry missions in Tarahumara-land, it has fallen into a state of considerable disrepair. Locals even use some of the side rooms as goat pens.

Four of us — a French-Canadian male, a French female, Gay and I — made the trip to Satevo one sunny scorcher of a December day. While the higher elevations of Copper Canyon Country were hunkering down in the throes of winter, we were wearing shorts and smearing on sunscreen. There is no winter in Batopilas Canyon.

The trail is an extension of the old Camino Real. Meaning it was designed for pack train use. Meaning it's a piece of cake to hike on.

We pulled out of Batopilas in the early afternoon, so we could hike back in the photogenic early evening. The walk was uneventfully wonderful, though we were filled with a modicum of apprehension because we were all so seriously psyched about visiting Satevo, which you can first see after the trail rounds a bend about a mile upriver from the mission.

The instant we arrived at the mission, a dozen or so children ran up, imploring us to purchase soft drinks from them. We had

Satevo Mission.

no idea there were stores in Satevo. Come to find out, there are two — each of which was represented by half the children. We ordered two soft drinks from one of the stores, and two more from the other. A few minutes later, the warm beverages were delivered, but the children refused to bring them to the mission steps, where we were sitting. They set them down outside the fence surrounding the mission. Okay, don't drink in church.

As we were sucking the drinks down, a couple of local baby-to-ting women came over. They asked if we wanted to take pictures of their offspring, certainly with the idea of charging us for each photo taken. It's hard to tell someone that you have no desire whatsoever to photograph their snotty-nosed little *niño*. But that's what we did. They walked away rejected. Asshole gringos!

When we entered the gloom of the mission, our pupils went on red alert. It was impossible, for the first few minutes, to see anything. So, do we stand there until our eyes adjust? No. That would be too smart. We immediately start poking around in some of the little side rooms. The first one, on the left as you walk in, is especially dank and dark. Stuck in one corner is a carved, wooden Tara ceremonial mask. In the darkness, the French-Canadian and I both thought it was a human head. We jumped about 17 feet in the air. Then, of course, being sensitive sorts of guys, we sent the females in without any warning.

There's a rickety ladder going up to the choir loft, which is about 40 feet above the main mission floor. We climbed up, as the ladder was shaking back and forth like a metronome. From the choir loft, you can, if you are stupid, ascend the bell tower. In addition to the fact that the bell tower looks like it could come separated from the mission at any moment with no external stimuli whatsoever, the ladder is a flimsy piece of kindling that is missing several steps. Then, to make matters even more interesting, if you fall, which you surely would, there's nothing to catch you until you reach ground level. We passed.

We hit the trail back to Batopilas about two hours before dark. On the way back, we stopped to take pictures on a rock outcropping above the river that affords a great view of the mission and a small suspension bridge. The evening colors lent a softness to the scene that, when you get right down to it, is anything but soft. Just about every plant in the area sports some manner of thorn. And the local fauna consists as much of rattlers and scorpions as it does Bambi and Thumper. But, this evening, the intense desert of the Batopilas Canyon seemed to mask its harshness well.

Come summer, certainly, such would not be the case. The temperatures this time of day would exceed 100 degrees F. The river would be in flood stage. The biting flies would be, well, biting. But right now, this is a little piece of heaven.

The best day-hike in Tarahumara-land.

PARTICULARS

Batopilas To Satevo Mission

You can easily make this trip without a map. It is almost impossible to get lost. If you would like to see where you are going on paper, get the 1:50,000 Batopilas topo. Satevo Mission is a little off that map, but not far. If you want to see the whole tamale, try to get a copy of the 1:50,000 Rio Batopilas topo. You may not have any luck.

Satevo Mission is two hours — about five miles — south of Batopilas. Just walk downriver from the town. If you stick to the riverbank, you will find yourself on the correct trail. Stay on the same side of the river as Batopilas all the way to Satevo.

Don't come here except in the dead of winter. Even then, you will be exposed to much direct sunlight.

There are two very small stores in Satevo, and plenty of campsites near the mission.

If you were of a mind to make this cakewalk into an intense backcountry experience, you could follow the Rio Batopilas south until it intersects with the Rio San Miguel, which is an extension of the Rio Verde. Hike up the San Miguel for a day and you will find yourself entering the Sinforosa Canyon of the Verde, the second-deepest canyon in the area. You can hike out to the village of Guachochi, which is connected by daily busses to Creel. You need to allow at least a week for this trip. Do not enter into it lightly. This is one of the most difficult trips in Tarahumara-land. Arrive on the scene physically prepared.

The trail from Batopilas to Satevo Mission is scheduled to be widened into a road, because a new silver mine is opening up in Satevo. Completion date is supposed to be early 1990. Though this project will certainly taint the trip described in this chapter, it will not ruin it. The area is too wonderful to be ruined. And, besides, this is Mexico. The road may never be built.

◄►

Gay negotiates the only rough section of trail
between Cerro Colorado and Munérachi.

14

Batopilas To Munérachi

I first heard about Munérachi from Lalo Valdez, the assistant manager of Las Cabañas del Cobre in Cusarare, who grew up in Batopilas. Lalo is one of the most wonderful people I have ever met, at least partially because he has the gift of being able to make his Spanish understandable to the Anglo ear. And he comprehends gringo babble. Meaning, when you talk to Lalo, you actually feel like you're making progress with your Español. He would make a great teacher.

Lalo told me that, in his opinion, the weirdest little mission town in Tarahumara-land is Munérachi (moo NAIR ah chee). Lalo and I had talked long into the night several times, in varying states of sobriety, about religion. We basically share the same non-beliefs, although I think Lalo is the more-confirmed theological skeptic. His favorite quote is from one of the recent Mexican presidents, who once said something like, "Mexico's problem is that it's too close to the United States and too far from God." Lalo takes it one step further. He thinks Mexico's problem is that it's too close to both the U.S. and God.

Lalo said that during the time that the Jesuits were ousted from Mexico, the Taras started modifying Catholicism. He added that in no other place in Tarahumara-land was that modification more evident than in Munérachi, which struck me as slightly strange because Munérachi is actually one of the most accessible Tara settlements in the Batopilas region. I would have thought that the weirdest aspects of Tarahumara-land would be found in the most boondock little corner of the most remote canyon. Munérachi is only about five or six nose-to-the-grindstone hiking hours from Batopilas. The hiking is very easy, however, along a trail that's as good as any I have ever hiked on.

There are several Mexican *ranchitos* along the way, but Munérachi is the first Tara turf you run into on this route. Lalo didn't really specify what manner of weirdness we might witness in the name of religion while visiting Munérachi, but one thing was for certain — I was not going to visit the Batopilas area without checking this place out. Strangeness in all its manifestations — good, bad and indifferent — is something that always merits investigation.

Lalo told me one other interesting thing about Munérachi. Apparently, there is a world-famous Tara musical group from there. Lalo said they're on the road nine months of the year and he didn't know if they would be home during our mid-December visit. From what I had heard in the way of indigenous Tara jams, at the very *least* I couldn't imagine a local combo traveling around the world giving concerts. I don't mean to put the Taras down on this. It's just that each culture has its positive and negative aspects and, somewhere along the line, some lines of artistic social evolution headed towards Tarahumara-land, while others headed to Vienna, the Andes and Nashville.

We were six on this three-day, two-night Batopilas to Munérachi round-trip: Andre, the same Canadian who accompanied us to Satevo Mission, Bob Gedekoh, an M.D. from Pittsburgh who wrote the Umira Bridge chapter, Mike Bush, an electrician from Ohio, Dean Fairburn, a student of the teaching arts from Knoxville, and Gay and I.

Bob, Mike and Dean, who had driven down from the States together, left their vehicle parked in Batopilas and simply began walking on the trail that starts right where the bridge crosses the river above town. The trail is on the same side of the river as Batopilas.

Andre, Gay and I drove back towards La Bufa, until we reached the turnoff for the *ranchito* of Casas Coloradas, about four kilometers from Batopilas. We asked one of the residents if we could park in his yard for a few days and, upon returning, paid him 10,000 pesos. This saved us about an hour of walking, although, of course, Bob, Dean and Mike made us feel guilty about being the lazy pieces of vermin we are.

We hiked from Casas Coloradas down to the Rio Batopilas,

pulled our boots off, crossed, sat down, put our boots back on,
hiked a few hundred feet, realized we still had to cross the stream
coming out of Arroyo Cerro Colorado, the side canyon we would
be hiking up, removed our boots, crossed and put our boots
back on again. That, right there, was the hardest part of this hike.
There are three trails heading up Arroyo Cerro Colorado towards Munérachi. One stays within 100 feet of the riverbed, and
the others are located on the two respective canyons walls, several
hundred feet above the river. During rainy season, the riverbed
route is impassable. The water level is so high that it's not possible
to cross from one side of the river to the other. Thus, there are
trail up high on both sides — so local commerce can still function.

Now, what I'm going to say is that the riverbed trail up Arroyo
Cerro Colorado is a can't-miss trail. But, understand before I do
so, that the six of us managed to miss it on several occasions on
the hike up. We'd be walking along a path so ragged a goat
would be embarrassed to be seen on it, all the while looking
over at this four-lane highway on the other side. We would scramble through the brush, down to the flood plain, cross the river
at a place with no good crossings, scramble up the other side,
only to realize several hundred yards later that, somewhere during all our scrambling, the good trail had crossed over to the
side we had just come from. This was more funny than bothersome and I have no excuses.

But, during one of these seemingly premeditated efforts to
avoid walking on the trail, we passed through a small Mexican
village that we would not have passed through otherwise, named
"Australia." I kid you not. There's a giant foundation of some
ancient edifice, which likely had something to do with the local
mining industry during its heyday 200 years back. We asked
several locals about the building, but none seemed to know its
history.

We returned to the trail by passing underneath an old water
viaduct, which is still being used for irrigation. It was so anti-
quated that it could have passed for something out of Italy. When
we got down to the river, we surprised eight or ten females,
who all looked related. They were doing laundry and taking
baths. One of the females, who looked about 16, was in a partial
state of undress. And she was very easy to look at. Until, that

is, the nuclear explosion of a spousal elbow impacted my rib cage.

When this underwear-attired nymph's grandmother — I guess it was her grandmother — realized there was a wife on the scene, the frightened look she sported when we first approached evaporated into a sly smile that spoke to the fact that all was well with the world.

Bob, Mike and Dean told us that they were planning to camp at the village of Cerro Colorado, where, they had heard, we would be able to buy soft drinks. Sounded like a good enough reason to camp there and we decided to join them.

Cerro Colorado — literally "red hill" — was located at the base of, you guessed it, a red hill, where active underground gold mining still takes place. It is about three hours hiking from Casas Coloradas, where we had parked our truck.

Placer mining also takes place on a small, though industrious scale, all along Arroyo Cerro Colorado. The ore is crushed in rounded, water-powered cisterns. Crude sluicing takes place after the ore is ground down.

Because of all the mining activity, the little creek flowing through Arroyo Cerro Colorado is bright red. In some places, it literally looks like a river of blood. The locals told us in no uncertain terms that the red water was not only fit for drinking, but it was *good* water. I stuck with bottled mineral water sold at the little store in town whenever I could.

Cerro Colorado is a real nice place. It has a main drag that almost feels like a little downtown. Of course, the main drag is also the *only* drag, but that just adds to the charm. The village has a decidedly tropical ambience. This is not surprising. It gets really hot in Cerro Colorado. Though it was getting close to Christmas, the daytime temperatures during our hike hovered in the low-90s F. When we mentioned to some Cerro Coloradans that it was hot, they laughed. When we mentioned that the flies were bothersome, they laughed. They bade us return sometime in the dead of summer to check out real heat and insect misery.

Several parties of gringos had passed through in the last three weeks, the store's proprietor, a reed-thin woman who had seen at least 200 summers, told us. She was tickled pink that business was booming. When she learned I was writing a book about the

Gay in beautiful downtown Cerro Colorado,
in front of the store.

area, she all but signed on to be my local agent. She had visions
of many, many soft drinks being sold in the future. I suggested
that she add some higher-octane beverages to her inventory. At
first, the thought seemed to intrigue her. Then it looked as though
she thought about the potential ramifications of having gaggles
of soused gringos hanging out in town and, well, it seemed like
she soured on the idea. Imagine that.

We camped right below town in a little field above the river.
Within a few minutes, we were entertaining visitors. Both the
mayor and the sheriff of Cerro Colorado dropped by for a chat.
Then some of the town's less-young, young ladies showed up.
The señoras at the store had noticed that there was only one
female among us and they commented on it. Being the only
member of the group able to utter so much as one syllable of
Spanish, I told them that our four comrades were all bachelors
and that they should pass the word that there were eligible
men-folk at-hand.

I walked down to camp, did a few chores and promptly forgot
all that babble about bachelorhood. Then, we started getting
visits from clusters of gussied-up 13-and 14-year-olds. I couldn't
figure it out at first. Suddenly, it dawned on me that this was

the local version of the parade of available material. This is not as sexist as it sounds. Well, yes, now that I think about it, it is as sexist as it sounds. Regardless, it is a fairly common occurrence in Mexico. Gay and I have witnessed it on a reasonably large scale, in Santiago Ixcuintla, near Tepic. Every post-pubescent un-married female in town was being led around by an older female while all the men in town stood on the sidelines with lecherous looks in their eyes. I mean, it was more innocent than this sounds. But, it amounts to the same thing.

The only problem was, all these young ladies were *young*. This is not to say that there weren't several of them who were very attractive. It's just that in Mexico, especially those parts like this one, where there are plenty of firearms for everyone, even an extended conversation with a señorita could get you "invited" to join the family, which maybe wouldn't be so bad.

Around dusk, all our visitors left. We all "snuck" down to the river to take a bath. There is a suspension bridge across the river, above flood level, connecting Cerro Colorado with the trail to the mine several thousand feet up the opposite side of the canyon. The locals must have been mighty curious for a goodly number of years as to gringo bathing techniques. The instant we hit the river sans garments, the town hustled out en masse onto the bridge, as well as the path above, to check out our soaping and rinsing procedures. At first, we tried to remain mostly underwater while we scrubbed. But this was December. The water was freezing. So, after a while the townsfolk were able to add to the local trove of knowledge concerning goose bump patterns on extremely white posteriors.

The next morning, we dropped our gear off at the store for safekeeping and headed out to Munérachi, about two hours away. We decided to stick to the river bottom and the hiking was very easy, with the exception of one place where we had to do a little simple scrambling.

We reached suburban Munérachi about noon. It is located in an idyllic spot at the confluence of two major arroyos. The mission is right next to a schoolhouse. There are a dozen or so Tara houses in the near vicinity. School was not in session, and the only adult near the mission was a Tara woman kneeling in the sunshine weaving a basket. A couple of her young children ran around playing. One, a little boy, about two, took one look at us and started screaming and crying.

The mission itself, this supposed bastion of Tara-modified Catholicism, was unoccupied. The six of us walked around in it for a while and were generally unimpressed, probably because only two days before, we had been in Satevo mission, which is the best one in Tarahumara-land. The floor of Munérachi mission was besmirched with several centuries worth of various types of animal droppings, covering the gamut from chicken to cow. Several ceiling beams in a side room were falling inward. The place had seen better days.

But there was no indication that any bizarre variety of Catholicism was practiced hereabouts. We were hoping at least for evidence of a sacrifice. Human skulls, something....

The only aspect of Munérachi that seemed out of the ordinary came in the form of two solar panels outside the school. I tried asking the woman weaving the basket if there was any live music to be had in the area, figuring that if there was a world-famous group headquartered here, everyone in town would know all about it. The woman looked at me like I was from Mars. She shook her head, then went back to her work. Oh well.

Since we had a multi-hour hike back to Cerro Colorado ahead of us, we didn't hang out too long. On the way back, the rest of the group made the mistake of actually thinking I knew where I was going. Since Munérachi is one of the destinations of those two trails that are several hundred feet above the river, they both descend to river level a few hundred yards south of the mission. I decided to check out the trail that was on the lefthand side as we were going downstream. Two feet from the river, it started heading intensely upward for about half a mile. I thought I heard the rest of the group say, as I was humping it up this incline, to hell with this, they were all going to return to Cerro Colorado the same way we had come — along the river.

I guessed correctly that the trail I was now on was going to pass by Cerro Colorado. I decided to hike very rapidly to get ahead of the group, so I could photograph them down on the river with Munérachi canyon in the background. This trail was a breeze. Once it topped out, about 400 vertical feet above the river, it was level to slightly downhill all the way to the point where it began switchbacking down to the river just above Cerro Colorado.

After about an hour, I stopped in the shadow of a spindly tree and rested. It was about 100 degrees F. Suddenly, I saw Andre rounding a corner about half a mile back. Then, one by one, came the rest of the gang. Though I was really enjoying the trail, I was afraid that everyone else would be displeased that I had led them away from the tranquility of the river. Quite the contrary. Everyone agreed that this stretch of trail was a nice change of pace. Though it was certainly more exposed to direct sunshine that the river trail, it provided more spectacular vistas.

We arrived back in Cerro Colorado in late afternoon. Everyone was ready for a cool dip and a cold beer. But, since there was no beer in town, we settled for 19 or 20 soft drinks each. We were all sunburned and seriously sweaty. Andre made arrangements to eat breakfast with the store's proprietors the next morning. They told us that for a small price they would be glad to feed us all, but the rest of us had plenty of food. Andre ended up with pinole, eggs and beans, which he enjoyed.

We set camp up, again, right below the store and hit the sack early. The night was very warm. I had carried neither a tent nor a winter bag and, for once, I didn't freeze my tail off.

The next morning on the way back out to Casas Coloradas, we passed a Tara man with a tumpline carrying a load of corn husks, which would be sold for goat food in Batopilas. This load extended about eight feet over the Tara man's head. It had to weight at least 200 pounds. The man said he had been walking all night. When we passed him, he looked tired, but he was still keeping up a fast pace.

A few minutes later, we passed a threesome of Mexican women, all wearing plastic sandals and sporting bright pink lipstick. They said good day to us. They ignored the Tara carrying the corn husks. And he ignored them. The peculiar harmony of Tarahumara-land. The cultural ballet of Copper Canyon Country.

▐▼▐▼▐▼▐▼▐▼▐▼▐ PARTICULARS **▐▼▐▼▐▼▐▼▐▼▐▼▐**

Batopilas To Munérachi

This whole route is located on the 1:50,000 Batopilas map.
Arroyo Cerro Colorado can be accessed by walking or driving
out of Batopilas. It is the first major side canyon on the left as
you are heading towards La Bufa on the road to Creel.
A trail leaves town on the same side of the river as Batopilas.
It begins at the bridge across the Rio Batopilas. This is a major
burro train trail. In about four easy kilometers, about an hour
on the trail, you will fork to the left, heading up the lefthand
side of a major side canyon — Arroyo Cerro Colorado. Just across
the Rio Batopilas is a cluster of houses. This is Casas Coloradas,
the place you would park your vehicle.

If you are driving, head out of Batopilas towards La Bufa. Take
the rugged-looking left four plus-or-minus kilometers from
Batopilas. Head down the hill until you come to a group of
houses. Ask if you can park there and offer to pay 5,000 pesos
a day. Cross the Rio Batopilas and cross the stream coming out
of Arroyo Cerro Colorado. Walk up the hill on the left side of
the arroyo and intersect the trail. The trail stays within 100 feet
of the riverbed, though there are trails on both sides of Arroyo
Cerro Colorado about 400 feet above the river. The river-level
trail crosses several times.

Simply follow this arroyo up for about three hours — about
five or six miles (eight or nine kilometers) — until you reach the
village of Cerro Colorado. For much of this walk, you will be
able to see Cerro Colorado, the hill. It is on the right (east) side
of the Arroyo Cerro Colorado as you are walking upstream. The
village of Cerro Colorado is on the left side. You will pass through
several other small Mexican villages between Casas Coloradas
and Cerro Colorado. Of particular interest is Australia because
of the ruins thereabouts.

From Cerro Colorado, where there is a small store owned by
the mother of the mayor, you continue up Arroyo Cerro Colorado
for about an hour until you reach an intersection of two giant
arroyos shaped like a "Y." Take the arroyo on the right. This is
Arroyo Munérachi, which leads all the way to Munérachi, another

two hours upriver.

There is also a trail connecting Munérachi and Cerro Colorado several hundred feet above the river. From Cerro Colorado, cross the swinging bridge and switchback up for half an hour until you come to a very well-worn trail. Take a left and walk for about two and a half hours to Munérachi.

From Munérachi, walk downriver a few hundred yards until you see a trail ascending the lefthand riverbank. Follow it up. The higher trail is completely dry and sports very little shade. This is some of the hottest territory in Tarahumara-land. Do not come here except in the dead of winter. Biting flies can be bad.

If you are looking for a longer hike, the Munérachi area offers up lots of possibilities. For instance, you can hike over to the village of Urique, located on the Urique River near the deepest section of canyon in Tarahumara-land. Urique is connected to the rim via a dirt road, which goes through Cerocahui, which has a hotel. You can either hike up this road or hitch. Traffic will be light. From Cerocahui, you can either hitch or hire someone to take you to the train.

View of Rio Conchos from Tehuirichi Mission.

15

Panalachi To Tehuirichi

At long last.

After four visits to Tarahumara-land, I finally find myself with an invitation to a *tesguinada* — a Tara corn beer bash. It's not much of an invitation, mind you. I mean, the head of the household where the festivities will be held did not send a runner to my residence bidding me to join the fun — which is the way it's usually done. Rather, it came from someone I rather doubt, in retrospect, was formally invited himself. But we won't nit-pick.

Gay and I had driven from Creel to the town of Panalachi, on the east side of the Continental Divide, by way of Bocoyna and Sisoguichi. This two-hour drive is one of the most pleasant I have ever experienced. Bocoyna, which is a Chihuahua-Pacific Railroad stop on the road that connects Creel and San Juanito, is a Mexican town near the headwaters of the Rio Conchos. It sports one of the oldest missions in Tarahumara-land, built in 1702.

At this point, the Conchos is but a trickle. The roads crosses it without a bridge, but even a passenger car could make the crossing with no sweat. This is the last we will see of the Conchos, though, until we arrive at the mission *ranchito* of Tehuirichi (tay wheer EE chee), the goal of this little excursion. By that time, it will be a fairly good-sized river.

We had been told by a Spaniard we met at Margarita's Guest House in Creel that the doctor in Panalachi would be happy to put us up for the night in his home, which also serves as the local hospital. Or, more accurately, the hospital also serves as his home. We remembered the health care facility we stopped at on our way back from Basaseachi Falls and decided, before the fact, that we would likely pass, even if we were offered a night's lodging.

Panalachi is an unusual town in that it is part Mexican and part Tarahumara. Usually, villages go one way or the other. It is also a fairly affluent looking place, dotted by numerous good-sized chalet-style dwellings.

We drank a couple of soft drinks in the morning sun in front of one of the town's several stores and asked about the doctor. The proprietor told us that we would be *expected* to stay at least one night at the hospital. We weren't planning on spending a night in town because it was early enough to hit the trail. But, we still needed a place to park the truck for the next few days. So, we drove up the hill to the doctor's residence.

We were at once surprised. This facility looked like a place where you could actually be treated and cured. The doctor, Alberto Sanchez, who was in his mid-30s, greeted us before we were even out of the truck. He told us that we couldn't have come at a better time because this was a fiesta/*tesquinada* day at Chacarachi, one of the local Tarahumara *ranchitos*. And, since he was invited, we were invited. Though we were very eager to get to the Conchos, a *tesguinada*, the backbone of any Tara fiesta worth its salt, was something we could not pass up. We asked several times if he was certain it would be okay for us to go to the fiesta. There was no doubt, Alberto responded.

Sanchez had been the sole health care professional in Panalachi for 12 years, as of late 1988. Like all Mexican doctors, he was required by law to spend his first year after graduation from medical school in a rural setting not of his choice. He was sent to Sisoguichi, which is a wonderful little mission town halfway between Bocoyna and Panalachi. He decided to stay in the area, not only because he liked the small-town ambience (he was born and raised in Mexico City), but because he thought there was a capitalist opportunity at hand. The locals, he said, though appreciative of the newly graduated doctors who blew in and blew out of town every year, were desirous of a more permanent situation.

So, Alberto decided to build his own hospital, though in Panalachi instead of Sisgoguichi because of cheaper land availability. It was a pure business decision undertaken without govern-

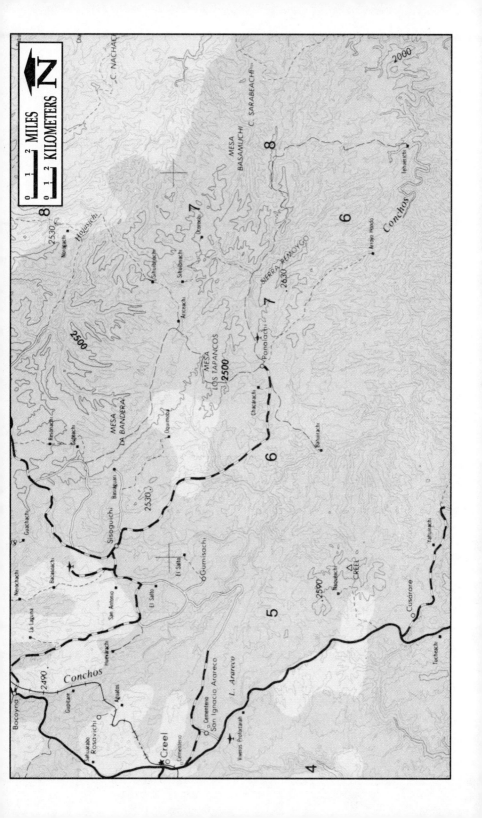

ment funds. It took a year to complete the hospital, which also houses living quarters for Alberto, his wife and child, who were off visiting relatives in Chihuahua City when we arrived. The place was well-stocked with equipment and medicines. We were offered use of the two-bed "ward" for the night.

Alberto was uncertain what time the *tesguinada* would begin, so we drove over to Chacarachi, only about two miles east of town, in early afternoon. Like most Tara *ranchitos*, Chacarachi is nothing more than a cluster of small dwellings. The residents were hard at it, getting ready for the *tesguinada*, which was being held because it was some local holiday.

The females of the *ranchito* were busy cooking the *tesguino* — in a full 55-gallon drum. This corn beer had been fermenting and cooking for a total of eight days. And it would have to be consumed within three days, because, after that, it would spoil. The females were also boiling up a vat of a dish that I am surprised has never become a mainstay of the American diet — cow blood. Ummmm.... Gay and I could barely keep from drooling all over ourselves.

Several local males were busy cutting up the carcass from which this blood had been drained. There was a mound of cow parts several feet high. Families that put on *tesguinadas* not only supply the beer, but the food as well. *Tesguinadas* generally last until all the beverages and victuals are gone.

Alberto seemed on friendly terms with all the residents of Chacarachi. Indeed, within two minutes, he had placed a food order with one of the resident females, who sort of rolled her eyes, smiled and went into one of the houses. Several minutes later, she came back out with a plate of cooked beef cubes and several blue corn tortillas.

Alberto ate the meal and then took us on a tour of *his* house, which came as something of a surprise. He was in the process of building a traditional Tara dwelling about ten feet from the rest of the houses in Chacarachi. He planned to use it as his weekend getaway, despite the fact that we were but ten minutes from his main house. Since it is illegal to sell *ejido* land, which certainly this was, we couldn't figure out how Alberto managed to wangle a house on Tara land. Perhaps he offered reduced-rate medical care to the residents of Chacarachi in exchange for them putting up with his non-Tara self.

The *tesguinada* wouldn't commence until about sundown that night, so we went back to the hospital for lunch and a siesta. We returned to Chacarachi about 7:00 p.m., finding our way through the dark by focusing on the four huge fires that were illuminating the *ranchito*. Wherever a group of Taras is gathered, there will always be more fires than it would seem necessary.

It is important to understand that *tesguinadas*, though punctuated by vast amounts of alcohol consumption, are ceremonial occasions. Thus, they have little in common with, say, a backyard barbecue during which a bunch of the boys get plowed on Budweiser while playing horseshoes. When we arrived, the local shaman was blessing the drinking circle — about 30 feet in diameter — which was marked out by rocks. He was chanting, dancing and waving a wand. The other eight or ten people gathered there were just sitting around staring into the huge bonfire, not paying much attention to the shaman.

We "shook" hands with everyone. The Tara "handshake" differs quite a bit from the American/European handshake, although, often, Taras will use our technique when meeting a gringo. They seem pleased when we know how to do it their way. They gently touch, just for an instant, the tips of each others' fingers, from about the second knuckle down, using the right hand.

It became obvious that our presence was unexpected, if not unwelcome. For one thing, *tesguinadas* are strictly sexually segregated. The females hang out around one fire, the males another. The fact that Gay was standing around the men's fire, which was about 50 yards from the houses we had visited that afternoon, seemed unsettling. The Tara men kept looking, not exactly viciously, but at least irritably, at her out of the corners of their eyes. So, we went with Alberto up to the women's fire, where the finishing touches were being put on the *tesguino*. Alberto joked around with the dozen or so women who were there — all of whom seemed a little flustered that there were two men and two Americans there. Alberto helped himself to some beef and popcorn. Then, he asked for a gourd, cut in half length-ways, out of which corn beer is always drunk. He dipped himself a gourdful out of a barrel, took a sip and passed it to us.

This is not the way it's usually done. One usually consumes *tesguino* while sitting around the officially designated drinking circle. The host starts things off by filling the gourd and handing it, first, to the eldest man there. After that, the gourd — and there's only one gourd per drinking circle (larger *tesguinadas* can have more than one circle) — is passed around. You are obligated to drink the entire gourdful, in one fell swoop, which is quite an accomplishment because these things hold at least a liter. When you're done, you stand up, walk over to the vat, refill the gourd and hand it to the next person. If you just hand the empty gourd back to whoever handed it to you, they will fill it back up and give it back to you.

It is not bad manners to leave the circle, but this is best done under the pretense of needing to relieve oneself, rather than, say, expressing a simple desire to split because you don't like the company. If you wish to drink no more mid-way through a gourdful of corn beer, there's a way out of it without losing too much face. All you need to do is spill the remaining *tesguino* all over your front and everyone there will laugh and think that you've just had a few too many. At this point, you will be relieved of your obligation to drink more when it's your turn again.

None of us had any desire to knock off that gourd of corn beer, even Alberto, who had mentioned earlier how he dislikes *tesguino*. A more foul beverage I had never tasted. I mean, mescal mixed with prune juice would be better than *tesguino*. I was disappointed. I guess I have this false image of myself as world-traveler that includes enthusiasm for all native alcoholic beverages.

We walked back to the men's fire with the now-half-empty gourd. The shaman was still doing his thing, meaning, in the eyes of tradition, the drinking lamp had not been lit. And, yet, there we were with a gourd of beer. We made banal chit-chat for an hour or so. Several of the men had wrapped themselves in their blankets and were dozing on the frozen ground. Since this party would last three days, maybe four, there was no hurry to get things moving. During that hour around the fire, I drank the rest of that gourd of corn beer. The more I drank, the better I liked it. I don't think I would ever order it in a bar, mind you, but it was better than I had first thought. At least, after a liter, that is. Gay, on the other hand, took a polite sip or two and vowed never to stray this far from Labatt's Blue again.

We headed back to the hospital before the party got going full-bore — seemingly much to the relief of our Tara hosts. On the way, we stopped at the home of a local guide. Alberto had been telling us all day that it would be impossible to find our way to Tehuirichi without a guide. When we told him that we thought we could make it alone, he acted insulted. So, we went along with it. He made all the arrangements, except for negotiating the price, while we sat in his van. He arranged for us to meet the guide at 10:00 the next morning.

This we did. The guide was a 70-year-old Mexican man with the most rotten teeth I have ever seen. He had a horse, which was saddled and ready to go when we arrived. A lever-action rifle was stuck into the scabbard. We asked if there was a reason for the weapon. He just shrugged and smiled.

During the five-minute walk from the hospital to the guide's house, we met a Canadian, Edmond Faubert, who is one of the best-known experts on Tarahumara arts and crafts. He helped author *The Other Southwest* with Bernard Fontana and Barney Burns and he obtained most of the items photographed in Fontana's book, *The Material Tarahumara*. In addition, he aided Fontana in his field work during the research phase of the *Tarahumara, Where Night is the Day of the Moon.*

Faubert was on his way to a small *ranchito* on the Conchos, where he hoped to buy a couple of pots. He offered us a ride to the top of the small ridge that lies between Panalachi and Tehuirichi, which is as far as the dirt road goes. We told the guide we would meet him on the other side. He hopped on his horse and rode out ahead of us, saying that he would be taking different route.

Faubert and his two Mexican companions dropped us off five miles later and we waited an hour for the guide. He never showed, so we began walking to Tehuirichi. We weren't exactly sad. Faubert had given us detailed directions and we had maps. This part of Tarahumara-land has little geographically in common with the rest. The Rio Conchos area has much gentler terrain. This is not to say it's like Nebraska. It's just easier to pick your way from one point to another without running into any 2,000-

foot cliffs.

We were told in Panalachi that it would take about three hours to hike to Tehuirichi. Faubert laughed. He said it would take us five hours from the place where he dropped us off. He warned us to always multiply by at least two the number of hours the Taras tell you it will take to walk some place.

Our plan was simple, though not complete. We wanted to walk to Tehuirichi and then back to Panalachi via a different route, if possible. Though not spectacularly beautiful in the same way that the deep canyons of Tarahumara-land are, the Conchos Valley is one of the highlights of Copper Canyon Country. There are only a few places where the Taras still live the same way they did 400 years ago. The Conchos is one of those places. You won't see many Taras dressed in K-Mart reject clothing in these parts.

At least three old Copper Canyon Country hands had told us that Tehuirichi was their favorite part of Tara-land. This area was all but unvisited by gringos as little as ten years ago. This is also the heart of Jesuit country. We were forewarned both by Skip McWilliams and Faubert that we would be made to feel very unwelcome by the priest and the two nuns who call Tehuirichi home. This is somewhat ironic because the Taras we ran into on this trip, both in Panalachi and on the trail to Tehuirichi, were the most friendly and outgoing we had met. They smiled easily and welcomed us to their territory. They seemed pleased that we were interested in visiting.

There are several trails from Panalachi to the Conchos, all of which are as good as any in Tarahumara-land. They are all de-signed for burro supply trains so they are well-graded and wide. From the point where Faubert dropped us off, we followed a trail that paralleled an arroyo that eventually intersects with the Conchos just south of the *ranchito* of Arroyo Hondo. (This is a different Arroyo Hondo than the one that intersects the Urique River near the village of Urique. "*Hondo*" simply means "deep.") At the site of an old abandoned mill, where there are several occupied Tara dwellings, we followed the wide path that started up the side of a ridge. Though it was December, the afternoon sun was harsh and hot. When we topped out on the ridge two miles later, the view of the Conchos Valley opened up to the south. It was a wonderful scene.

*View of
Tehuirichi
Mission
from
Rio Conchos.*

It was here that we made a small directional mistake. We should have followed this ridge down towards the Conchos. But, the grand trail we had been following continued southeast into another arroyo. The trail that followed the ridge directly to Tehuirichi was faint as it exited from the trail we had been following. We didn't know this until our return trip two days later. This presented no real problem. Quite the contrary. Instead of following the same trail both directions, we ended up finding a nice little loop.

The trail we followed went straight down into the arroyo, which was, at this point, only about 300 feet deep. The rock formations we passed beneath were spectacular. About six or eight miles later — three hours past the point where the trail topped the ridge — we found ourselves on a small bluff overlooking a trickle of a river that was the Conchos. We had expected something a little larger. This thing was much smaller than Cusa-rare Creek. But the volume wasn't the only "problem." The river seemed to be flowing in the wrong direction. The Conchos flows directly east for several hundred miles until it joins the Rio Grande at Presidio, Texas. This section was flowing almost due west. We hiked down the bluff into one of the most beautiful flood plains I had ever seen. The tall grass was golden in the late afternoon sun. There were several abandoned Tara home-steads on the hills near the river. We had been told that Tehuirichi, which we thought this cluster of houses was, was almost totally — albeit temporarily — abandoned, due to a very poor corn harvest the year before. The residents were mostly in Chihuahua City and Juarez — begging their way through the winter.

Gay wandered off to take pictures while I strolled down to the river with the water pump. Purifying water is, without a doubt, the worst camp chore there is. I own a Katadyn filter, which is the bee's knees of backpacking water pumps. It is still a drag to use, as are all other types and models. The few companies that manufacture backpacking water pumps all say stuff like "...purifies a liter of water is 90 seconds." My ass. I think they arrive at those figures by putting professional wrestlers in the middle of the Sahara for three waterless days and then promising them all the cold beer they can drink if they can pump a liter of water through one of these buggers in 90 seconds. And, even then, if they tried to pump second and third liters through in the same amount of time, they would fail. I estimate that it takes me about five or six minutes per liter, which is a drag when you find yourself going through several gallons a day per person.

But slow pumping was the least of my worries this fine even-ing. I couldn't get over the fact that the damned river was flowing the wrong way. I pulled out my map and compass and oriented and re-oriented them. Nothing, including the possibility that we were in the middle of a huge yazoo-type bend, would explain the matter.

A couple of male Taras passed, dressed in their traditional white dress-looking garments. I ran over and asked them if this was the Conchos and if this was Tehuirichi. Yes, they said, this was the Conchos, but Tehuirichi was a few kilometers downriver.

Once again, due primarily to chronic laziness, I did not tote a tent. And, once again, we froze. Though I knew the Conchos Valley was nowhere near as deep as Copper Canyon, I was operating under the assumption that the temperatures would be warmer here than in Panalachi. We awoke to the heaviest frost I have ever seen — and I have wintered in the Colorado mountains. Our bags were soaked through. It took until 11:00 in the morning to get them dry, which was no problem because we only planned on hiking as far as Tehuirichi.

The hike down the Conchos was a cakewalk. The trail was perfect, the sunshine warm and the scenery splendid. The valley at this point was perhaps 1,500-feet deep, with rounded hills bounding it, punctuated by occasional cliff faces. Gay said later that this was her favorite stretch of trail in all of Tarahumara-land. We had to cross the river a few times, but, since the water was so shallow, those crossings were easy.

After an hour, we started passing a few more Tara orchards and houses. I yelled up a hill to a couple of Taras who were building a chicken coop, asking them if this was Tehuirichi. They said it was. We rounded a bend and the mission came into sight. But that wasn't all. A big river, at least 50 yards wide, also came into sight. The Tara men I had talked to last night must have misunderstood my question. The creek we had camped next to was not the Conchos afterall, just a small tributary, which explained why it was flowing the wrong way with so little water.

There was a school near the mission. As we passed, dozens of Tara children came pouring out to watch us. We waved. No response. We yelled *"cuira"* (koo EE rah) — Tara for "hello." Again, no response. The friendliness we had experienced over the last few days was not in evidence in Tehuirichi. We had been told that the resident Jesuits would watch you die of thirst on their front porch before offering you a glass of water. Perhaps they preached the doctrine of standoffishness to their local flock.

We plopped our packs right in the mission courtyard. One of the resident nuns walked around a corner just as we arrived. She tried to ignore us, but I wouldn't let her. I asked where we could camp. We could tell from the look on her face that she did not relish the thought of having us for neighbors, even for one night. She pointed, in response, north, towards Panalachi. Actually, I was joshing with her. We had decided, since it was getting colder than we had expected, to head back towards Panalachi that night.

We went down to the river to fill our water bottles, and were joined by two young Tara boys — about ten years old — who were, likewise, on water detail. I asked, in Spanish, if they spoke Spanish. They both shook their heads, meaning they understood at least a little. A few minutes later, one of them shyly asked if I had any *dulces* — Spanish for "candy." I responded that I thought they didn't speak any Spanish. They giggled at being found out. We chatted for a few minutes before they headed up towards the school with a full bucket of water.

Gay and I ate lunch next to the mission. The nun pointed to the arroyo behind the mission when we asked her what the most direct route back to Panalachi was. We left, hoping to camp at the abandoned sawmill near where Edmond Faubert had dropped us off the day before. A few minutes out of Tehuirichi, we passed a Tara woman who was returning from the *tesguinada* we had been to. She was in bad shape, with dried *tesguino* all down her chin and the reddest eyes this side of Mardi Gras. She was staggering and looked like she had the worst hangover in the history of the world. She was friendly, though. She had heard about the gringos who had crashed the party, sort of chuckling as she said this.

The hike back was surprisingly difficult, at least partially because we lost the trail. This was frustrating because this is a well-traveled route. An hour north of Tehuirichi, we found ourselves looking down a small cliff. I think this is where the trail and us went separate directions. I climbed down a rickety wooden ladder. Gay went off in search of an easier way. This transpired at the edge of a Tara *ranchito* and the whole clan came out to watch the gringos. They were laughing and pointing. Once again, we were the entertainment.

After following a goat path for several miles, we finally hooked back up with the main trail. This must have been the route that Faubert had described to us. He had mentioned that we would be passing some of the most interesting rock formations in the region, which we did — dark Precambrian-looking spires several hundred feet tall that seemed straight out of some old caveman movie. The trail followed a ridge that sported a fascinating butte that we had seen from a distance on our way down the day before. From higher up, you can see the flat top of this butte. It looks putting green smooth. The trail skirted the cliffs that formed the base of this butte, which was about 100 feet higher than the ridge at this point. The top seemed inaccessible.

Once again, the late afternoon sunlight was lip-scorching hot. Much of this trail was shadeless, with short little ups and downs, the most-tiring kind of hiking. We intersected with the trail we had followed the day before just as the sun was sinking over the Continental Divide. At this point, we were only about 15 minutes from the place we wanted to camp, so Gay stayed behind to take pictures while I went ahead to set up camp. I didn't want to camp right in the backyards of the Tara shacks near the old mill site, so I walked about 100 yards up the arroyo and laid my pack right in the middle of the trail, which, at this point, was as wide as a road. It was also the only flat spot around. By the time Gay caught up with me, I had our little love nest set up with dinner — home-dried chile — bubbling on the stove.

It took us about three easy hours to hike back to Panalachi the next morning, via the same dirt road we had ridden over with Faubert. We stopped by the residence of our "guide." His wife came running out with tears in her eyes, thanking God that we were alive. The same thing for the guide. Apparently, the old man had misunderstood where he was supposed to meet us, which wouldn't have been hard because we, having never been there before, weren't exactly specific. He had spent almost 24 hours combing the woods looking for us, returning home only after he was convinced we were dead. He and his wife were trying to decided whether to call the army in to look for our corpses. We went ahead and paid him the same as if he had led us by the hand to Tehuirichi and back.

On our way out of town, we drove by Chacarachi. The *tesguinada* was still going strong. We considered stopping by again, but thought better of it. We could wait until we reached Bocoyna, the closest place where we could buy gringo beer. A little less romantic, perhaps, but much easier on the tongue and stomach.

▐▞▚▞▚▞▚▞▚▞▚▌ PARTICULARS ▐▞▚▞▚▞▚▞▚▞▚▌

Panalachi To Tehuirichi

You will need to rely on the 1:250,000 San Juanito map. Panalachi is on the 1:50,000 Creel map, but Tehuirichi is not. It is doubtful you will be able to buy the 1:50,000 Norarachi topo, which contains Tehuirichi, in Creel. Try at the Mission Store.

The most difficult part of this hike is access. There is no public transportation to Panalachi. You could hire a taxi in Creel, but this will likely prove expensive. If you can get to Bocoyna by train or by hitching from Creel, you should be able to hitch southeast to Panalachi. The dirt road, which is in pretty good shape, is traversed by many logging trucks. It could take you more than a day, however, if traffic is light. Halfway between Bocoyna and Panalachi is the town of Sisoguichi, which has a nice hotel and an old mission. I have seen advertisements for tours to Sisoguichi at Margarita's and the Parador in Creel. You could sign up for one of these and hitch the rest of the way. Or you could ask Margarita or the Parador to put together a custom tour for you all the way to Panalachi. To save money, this is better done with several people.

Panalachi can also be accessed by hiking from Cusarare and Tehuirichi can be accessed from Choguita. (Chapter 7)

There are no hotels in Panalachi, though the local doctor, Alberto Sanchez, rents out the traditional Tara house he has built at Chacarachi, which is only a few minutes out of town. Anyone in Panalachi can point you to the hospital where Alberto lives. We were invited to stay in the hospital, but you shouldn't go to Panalachi expecting the same offer, especially if tourism picks up in this area.

The trail to Tehuirichi goes over the ridge east of town. You can see the trail from the hospital. Hike over that ridge, a distance of about five miles (eight kilometers), heading down the arroyo on the other side. This arroyo will take you all the way to the Rio Conchos, about five more miles, via the *ranchito* of Arroyo Hondo. There is a good trail. You can hike downriver from there to Tehuirichi — again, about five miles away.

Or, from the arroyo, you can hike up the ridge directly to the east. Before ascending, hike down the arroyo until you come to a cluster of Tara houses, located at the site of an old abandoned sawmill. You will see a distinct trail switchbacking up the ridge. Follow this trail down the ridge to a saddle, about two miles from the houses. Here, you have two choices. You can continue on the east side of the ridge, skirting the beautiful butte you will see to the south from here. The trail will, at first, be a little hard to find, but it leads right to Tehuirichi.

Or, you can bypass the ridge trail and keep following the main trail down into the next arroyo to the east. This arroyo intersects a small creek after about five miles. Follow this creek downstream — to the west — for a mile or two. It will interest with the Rio Conchos at Tehuirichi. From there, you can follow the arroyo directly behind the mission back towards Panalachi. Or, you can head upriver for five miles or so until you come to Arroyo Hondo. Follow this north until you meet the main trail to Panalachi.

Though the Conchos is not as tough as, say, the Urique, it will still be a rough slog if you decide to follow it any distance. You will have to cross it many times. And you will be walking on sand with wet boots the rest of the time.

You would be well-advised to day-hike around Panalachi. This little town is located in a beautiful high valley worthy of exploration.

There are several small stores in Bocoyna, Sisoguichi and Panalachi, but nothing in Tehuirichi.

◄►

Huddling beside the campfire near Tehuirichi.

Epilogue

J ust last week, I interviewed a professional kayaking/rafting guide who plies his trade on the Arkansas River near where I live. This guy looks to be about 50. He was a schoolteacher for 20 years and is spending his "retirement" working as a salaried river rat. An educated man, with enough years under his belt to have developed perspective.

The photographer who was with me asked this man if he had kayaked "all over the world." Fundamental enough question. The answer, surprisingly, was an emphatic "no." Not intoned in an unfriendly fashion, mind you. Stated just strongly enough that there was no doubt as to where this man was coming from. He went on to tell us that, in his opinion, Americans should not recreate themselves in the third world, for reasons unexplained. Overlooking for a moment that there are plenty of places "all over the world" that are not third world — Australia and Norway come to mind — where one *could* kayak, were they so disposed, I was, nonetheless struck. Even though we didn't pursue the subject, the timing could not have been worse.

The very day before this conversation took place, I had, essentially finished this book with the exception of the epilogue. At the same time that I was seriously pumped at the thought of having this project behind me, I was — and still am — very nervous about its potential negative implications for the Tarahumaras and their turf. The conversation with the kayaker did not help matters any, because, I suspect, his reasoning was based on the "fact" that "we" inevitably adversely impact the "primitive" cultures that oftentimes serve as ambience-enhancement units in the boondock locales we backpack through in the name of R & R.

It's not like this is something I have never mentally dealt with before.

Publisher Walt Borneman and I both believe that this book is primarily reactive, in the sense that tourism is already on the increase in Tarahumara-land. But it is not lost on us that these words will likely also prove to be proactive, insofar as they will encourage certain numbers of visitors, who otherwise might never have heard of Copper Canyon Country, to check the place out. As well, it may well encourage visitors who otherwise might never have ventured farther than the Chihuahua-Pacific train to hoist their packs and head out into the backcountry.

Meaning, because of my work, the Tarahumara culture will come in contact with more outsiders than it would if I had just gone ahead and fallen off that cliff in Tararecua Canyon, my chips cashed in five years before penning this work.

Okay, so I am a pimp, of sorts. I take the money while Copper Canyon Country takes the physical impact. I can live with that. Because, as such, I can get away with admonishing visitors to use cultural condoms during all social intercourse with Tarahumara-land. And because I agree with Skip McWilliams that the Taras are already being raped by the Mexican timber industry. Therefore, the Tara culture might actually *need* gringo backpackers to come tromping through their backyards in ever-increasing numbers. Granted, that provides fairly good rationalization for one who may be searching pretty desperately for just that. But it's good rationalization. And, it's rationalization necessitated by the axe, the chainsaw and the pesos they provide.

Backpackers give — or will give — the Tara culture an economic alternative. The Tarahumara culture has entered the 20th century. It has entered the monied economy. There is no turning back the clock on either of those realities. And, even if there was, it would not be up to us to do the turning back. The Tarahumaras are hunters and gatherers. They are enjoying the gathering potential of that which the 20th-century, monied economy offers. They still seem to prefer their own culture, and their culture is strong enough to "ward off" — for lack of a better term — those aspects of outside cultures that they don't like.

At the same time, of course, gringos armed with cash and

trinkets are materialistically strong enough to overcome even the most determined resistance.

It seems inevitable. Once a place gets hot on the tourist circuit, it's only a matter of time before people start saying how "you should have been here ten years ago." I wish I knew for certain that Tarahumara-land will not suffer from its newfound popularity. Historic precedence indicates that it is already too late. You know, once the first American or European comes walking into camp, you might as well sell your cultural stock because, from then on, it's a bear market, whether you're dealing with missionaries, loggers or... backpackers.

If there is a chance for a different scenario, Tarahumara-land is it. It has everything necessary to maintain its cultural integrity while, concurrently, allowing outsiders to share in its majesty. The Taras own their land communally. They have a rock solid culture mostly resistant to and distrustful of external influences. They have independent-thinking individuals who, on the whole, prefer remaining true to themselves. Combine that with extreme minimum-impact visitations on our part and, *for once*, there may be no head-hanging 20 years down the road. Not for the gringos. And not for the Taras.

Amen and Miller time....

Cañon City, Colorado
April 9, 1989

◄►

Acknowledgements

The "job" — hey, someone's gotta do it — of researching this book would have been much more difficult were it not for the help provided me by the owners and staff of Las Cabañas del Cobre in Cusarare, Chihuahua, Mexico: Suzanne McWilliams, Skip McWilliams, Oscar Loya, Lalo Valdez, Pepe and Oralia Castro Olivas, Aida Olivas, Rafael Morquecho and the "Mexican Gandalf," Jesus Manuel Olivas. These people have given me a place to call home in Tarahumara-land and I thank them.

I would also like to thank Dr. Robert Gedekoh, of Elizabeth, Pennsylvania, for providing the text on the Umira Bridge-Urique Narrows hike.

◄►

Annotated Bibliography

Abbey, Edward. *Abbey's Road*. New York: Dalton, 1979. One chapter on Copper Canyon Country. Not very good.

Artaud, Antonin. *The Peyote Dance*. New York: Farrar, Strauss and Giroux, 1976. English translation of "Les Tarahumaras." Last half was written from the author's digs in a French psycho-ward. Very weird.

Bennett, Wendell, and Zingg, Robert. *The Tarahumara, an Indian Tribe of Northern Mexico*. Glorieta, New Mexico: Rio Grande Press. A scientific study of the Taras and Tarahumara-land.

Bradt, Hilary, and Rochowiecki, Rob. *Backpacking in Mexico and Central America*, Cambridge, Massachusetts: Bradt Enterprises, 1982. (95 Harvey Street, Cambridge, Massachusetts 02140). Contains but one chapter about Copper Canyon Country — actually guest-written by A. R. Alexandrocvich — but, it's a good chapter. Nice book for getting an overview about hiking in Latin America.

Boudrea, Eugene. *Move over, Don Porfirio: Tales from the Sierra Madre*. Sebastopol, California: Pleasant Hills Press.

Boudrea, Eugene. *Trails of the Sierra Madre*. Capra/Scrimshaw, 1973.

Carlson, George. *A Tarahumara Portfolio*. Reno, Nevada: University of Nevada Press, 1983.

Cassel, Jonathon F. *Tarahumara Indians*. San Antonio, Texas: Naylor Corp., 1969.

Dunne, Peter Masten. *Early Jesuit Missions in Tarahumara*. Berkeley, California: University of California Press, 1948.

Fisher, Richard. *National Parks of Northwest Mexico*. 3rd Ed. Tucson, Arizona: Sunracer Publications, 1988. (P. O. Box 40092, Tucson, Arizona 85717). The author, a professional guide/backcountry photographer, provides us with good art and sensitive observations.

Fontana, Bernard. *Material World of the Tarahumara*. Tucson, Arizona: Arizona State Museum, 1979. Great overview of Tara arts and crafts.

Fontana, Bernard. *Tarahumara, Where Night is the Day of the Moon.* Flagtaff, Arizona: Northland Press, 1979. Ethnological observations augmented by good photography.

Fontana, Bernard; Burns, Barney; and Faubert, Edmond. *The Other Southwest.* Phoeniz, Arizona: Heard Museum, 1977.

Forgey, William, M.D. *Wilderness Medicine,* Merrillville, Indiana: ICS Books, Inc., 1987. (One Tower Plaza, Merrillville, Indiana 46410) The best book I have ever seen to prepare backcountry users for that which we all hope never happens — a wilderness medical problem.

Franz, Carl. *The People's Guide to Mexico.* Santa Fe, New Mexico: John Muir Publications. (P. O. Box 613, Santa Fe, New Mexico 87504) Simply the best book ever penned about general travel in Mexico. As a matter of fact, one of the best travel books period. Doesn't deal with Tarahumara-land, but deals with everything else about the country. A great read even if you never venture south of the border.

Ilg, Steve. *The Outdoor Athlete.* Evergreen, Colorado: Cordillera Press, Inc., 1987. Everything the backpacker needs to know about preparing physically. Contains sport-specific exercise regimens.

Kennedy, John. *Tarahumara of the Sierra Madre: Beer, Ecology and Social Organization.* Arlington Heights, Illinois: AHM Publishing Corporation, 1978.

Kennedy, John. "Bonds of Laughter Among the Tarahumara Indians: A Rethinking of Joking Relationship Theory," in *The Social Anthropology of Latin America — Essays in Honor of Ralph Leon Beals.* Los Angeles: Latin America Center, University of California, 1970.

Kennedy, John, and Lopez, Raul. *Semana Santa in the Sierra Tarahumara: Comparative Study in Three Communities.* Los Angeles: Museum of Cultural History, University of California, 1981.

Lumholtz, Carl. *Unknown Mexico, Explorations in the Sierra Tarahumara and Other Regions, 1890-1898.* Glorieta, New Mexico: Rio Grande Press. Considered the bible of Tarahumara-land.

Roca, Paul. *Spanish Jesuit Churches in Mexico's Tarahumara.* Tucson, Arizona: Univeristy of Arizona Press, 1979.

Schultheis, Rob. *The Hidden West.* Berkeley, California: North Point Press, 1983. Again, but one chapter. Interesting observations by the author of *Bone Games.*

Sheridan, Thomas E., and Naylor, Thomas H. *Raramuri — a Tarahumara Chronicle, 1607-1791.* Flagstaff, Arizona: Northland Press, 1979.

◄►

Index

◄►

About The Author

M. John Fayhee is a contributing editor to *Backpacker* and a veteran outdoor writer whose articles on adventure travel all over the world have appeared in *Backpacker, Adventure Travel, Canoe Magazine* and numerous regional publications. When not on the road, Fayhee lives near the Arkansas River in southern Colorado with his wife, Gay Gangel-Fayhee.

While *Mexico's Copper Canyon Country* is his first published book, he has four others in the works: "A. T. Debauched," about his unfocused, five-month, end-to-end hike on the Appalachian Trail back in the days before he understood that liver transplants are costly, to say nothing of brain transplants; "The Urban Environmentalist's Survival Manual;" "Mountain Biker's Mexico;" and a novel, "Ace."

Beginning in the fall of 1989, Fayhee will be guiding trips into and through Copper Canyon Country. For information, contact Fayhee at 245 N. Raynolds Avenue, Cañon City, Colorado 81212, (719) 275-3619. Fayhee is also available for film presentations about his Tarahumara-land forays.

◄►

Other Outdoor Guides From Cordillera Press

ARIZONA'S MOUNTAINS
A Hiking and Climbing Guide
Bob and Dotty Martin

COLORADO'S CONTINENTAL DIVIDE
A Hiking and Backpacking Guide
Ron Ruhoff

COLORADO'S HIGH THIRTEENERS
A Climbing and Hiking Guide
Mike Garratt and Bob Martin

TAKE 'EM ALONG
Sharing the Wilderness with Your Children
Barbara J. Euser

THE OUTDOOR ATHLETE
Total Training for Outdoor Performance
Steve Ilg

THE SAN JUAN MOUNTAINS
A Climbing and Hiking Guide
Robert F. Rosebrough

◄►